WHAT IF?

Ideas on Creation,
Our Universe,
Our Life,
How We Got Here,
and How We Get Home!

CHARLEE STARDUST

BALBOA.PRESS
A DIVISION OF HAY HOUSE

Balboa Press books may be ordered through booksellers or by contacting:

Balboa Press
A Division of Hay House
1663 Liberty Drive
Bloomington, IN 47403
www.balboapress.com
844-682-1282

Because of the dynamic nature of the Internet, any web addresses or links contained in this book may have changed since publication and may no longer be valid. The views expressed in this work are solely those of the author and do not necessarily reflect the views of the publisher, and the publisher hereby disclaims any responsibility for them.

The author of this book does not dispense medical advice or prescribe the use of any technique as a form of treatment for physical, emotional, or medical problems without the advice of a physician, either directly or indirectly. The intent of the author is only to offer information of a general nature to help you in your quest for emotional and spiritual well-being. In the event you use any of the information in this book for yourself, which is your constitutional right, the author and the publisher assume no responsibility for your actions.

Images created by Charlee Stardust

THE HOLY BIBLE, NEW INTERNATIONAL VERSION®, NIV® Copyright © 1973, 1978, 1984, 2011 by Biblica, Inc.® Used by permission. All rights reserved worldwide.

Print information available on the last page.

ISBN: 978-1-5043-8945-7 (sc)
ISBN: 978-1-5043-8946-4 (hc)
ISBN: 978-1-5043-8947-1 (e)

Library of Congress Control Number: 2017915292

Balboa Press rev. date: 11/13/2020

IN MEMORIAM

I owe the finishing of this writing in large part to the love of my life, Buddy, my companion of twelve years. In the fall of 2015, his work was done here as he made his transition into his next life. This work is dedicated to him, with all my love, heart, and soul, for all the joy!

CONTENTS

FOREWORD

Our world is a magnificent place, full of everything imaginable, and why not? We imagined it! We can imagine joy or sorrow, love or hate. We have the free will to choose what to make of it, the good, the bad, and the ugly of it. We are programmed to feel alive by the drama of it. The pages herein will, I trust, illustrate, at least from my perspective, the why of it.

This book was written with much love.
Charlee

INTRODUCTION

My name is unimportant. After all, what's in a name? Doesn't a rose, by any other name, smell as sweet? Still, we humans like to name things, and we like to refer to each other by name. Therefore, if you must have a name for me, you may call me Charlee or Starry or anything you like; just, please, don't call me late for dinner!

While maturing through my early adulthood, it was obvious that I had significant opinions about life, religion, our Universe, and most surely about God. Many deep discussions about such ensued with close family and friends which sparked requests for me to write my thoughts down so that they could be better understood by everyone. I complied, and began a joyful quest to illuminate my ideas in more detail.

As I wrote this collection of my deepest thoughts and ideas, I kept returning to the question; *what if?* What if God is real? What if Heaven is real? What if frogs had wings (my mother would say)? As I tried to resolve conflicting opinions about all thing worldly, that reflection created even more what-if questions and my mind expanded to take on the challenge of answering even the seemingly ridiculous question of which came first, the chicken or the egg?

Over the years, I have tried to make sense of our world and the difference between this world and the world of God, our Creator. I conclude that they both cannot be real, existing in the same space in time, because they are diametrically opposed to one another. The realm, or the place that God resides, has to be pure, perfect, full of love, comfort, joy and bliss, or so I would imagine. Our world is mad, chaotic, imperfect, and full of fear, leading to hatred, suffering, war, and death. Therefore, one world has to be a false world. This startling conclusion troubled me for many years, for it also meant that God could not have created our world. I wanted to believe in God, but my loving God would never create such ugliness for his beloved to experience. There had to be another answer!

I began to reason that our physical world must be an alternate reality. But, how did it come about, and why? So began my quest to answer the larger, seemingly unanswerable, thought-provoking questions. What created our world, our Universe? Where did we really come from? What is our purpose here? Is it just me, or is it human nature to question our existence?

What if we are not who we think we are? What if this false alternate reality is like a movie and we are simply taking on the role of acting out in it? Let's call this movie The Great Contrast, an epic adventure of what it would be like to experience life in a physical world. What if we divvied parts in this movie, where some of us play the director, some producer, some set designer, inventor, stagehand, lead actor, and so on? What if we are really one, playing all these roles? On the other hand, what if this is all just a big dream, a nightmare, perhaps?

If God didn't create this place, then who or what did and for what purpose? Since we are so intricately involved in this world, we must have had a hand in creating it, regardless of whether you believe this is an epic movie or a dream! But who are we? What does it mean to be mortal or human? What do we really know about life and about death?

What If We Never Really Die?

Most of us have wondered what happens when we die. What happens to *me*? Surely, my body will eventually die. Then what? There are some people, like my father, who believed that this is all there is, and when we die, that's it, we are done, no more. People like my father, who are so heavily invested in identifying with the physical body, believe in the I-am-my-body concept. It is easy to understand that, when people think of the physical body no longer functioning, that would be the end of us. And, of course, there are those who believe in a biblical God and the notion that if you are good, your spiritual essence will go to a place called Heaven, when you die, and be reunited with our Creator. And if you are not good, you may go to a place called Hell, or, sit in Purgatory, until God judges your life. I know many people who genuinely believe this, but this always troubled me.

I would eventually reason that if both ideas did exist, neither Heaven and Hell are physical places, so you do not go anywhere when your physical body stops functioning. Your soul, the real you, simply changes its state of consciousness. What our consciousness experiences at that point is strictly up to our prior memories or perceptions from the physical world we inhabited, while our physical host bodies were alive. Heaven and Hell are simply constructs that we humans have concocted to explain what happens next, and, perhaps, to police our behavior while we are living out this experience. And that's all life on earth is, just an experience. The good news is that there is a Heaven. However, getting back to that place which has no place will not be easy. After finishing this work, you will, perhaps, understand how and why, from my perspective at least. And while it is predicted that it won't be easy to get back to Heaven, it is, however, doable, and it will be the most joyous of reunions with our Creator! You should note that much of my perspective on this topic stems from the insights I gleaned from *A Course In Miracles*, which I will highlight a little later on in this text.

Spirits Incarnate

More and more humans are of the mind-set that we are more than our physical bodies. In fact, entire cultures and religions believe in reincarnation. Those who believe that we have been here before also believe that we are not our physical bodies, but spirits incarnate. Therefore, the *I* and the *we* in our conversations must be spiritual and not physical. The problem is that most people stop short of spiritual identification, because they have difficulty disassociating with the physical body. Herein lies the problem.

If you study people who associate more with their spiritual bodies than they do their physical bodies, you will most likely find people who have more peace and contentment than those who spend all their attention on the physical. The reason is because most of our dramas in life spawn from our heavy association with the physical. When you embrace your spiritual being, you are happier because you can live more fully in the moment. You find joy in the smallest places. You are less likely to live in fear, because you do not dwell on what the future may bring. You live in the here and now. Eckhart Tolle writes beautifully about this in his work *The Power of Now*.

When you live more fully in the now moment, you also have fewer regrets and find it easier to release concerns of the past. When you see drama in someone, either they are dwelling upon something in the past (recent or long ago, makes no difference), or they are fretting over something that has not yet happened. They are not living in the now moment. Realize how ridiculous it is to dwell upon something that has already taken place, something which you cannot change. Likewise, worrying about something that has yet to happen is equally a waste of valuable time. Drama is always self-induced, brought on by our minds ability to create a story about something we are pondering. Often times that story gets out of hand and produces drama that we feel must be played out. And so we do. We are always active participants in our drama, but we generally do not produce a solo performance because our ego wants other actors involved. So the director in us (our ego) will seek out others to play a role in our drama in order to keep it alive.

Living in the now moment enables us to disassociate with our physicality, and to a certain degree from our ego, and we are less likely to worry about dying because we understand that we are something more than our bodies. Therefore, we never really die.

Think of it this way. You are an inventor (and we all are). You invent a great vehicle. You pride yourself on making it unique and one of a kind. You love this vehicle because it is something that you created and it works well for you. You use this vehicle for many years, but over time parts begin to wear out and break down. Because you are so attached to this vehicle, you replace those parts in an attempt to maintain it and keep it functioning. You are comfortable in this vehicle and you make improvements to its design so that it might last longer. Then, one day, an accident happens and it is destroyed. It is a total loss and, sadly, you must say goodbye and have the vehicle hauled off to a cemetery. You obtain or create another vehicle to take its place and the cycle continues.

Understand that we are all Creators. As easy as it is to invent or create a new automobile, we could also be responsible for creating the physical human body for the same reason; we needed a vehicle in the world of form. Think about it. We had all the motive, if our intention was to experience a life of contrast, which is something Heaven lacks. We are explorers by nature of our reason for creating contrast. We wanted to explore all that we could imagine. We created the human body to use as a vehicle for our true selves, our spirits, to experience the wondrous contrast that we have created. We pride ourselves on making the body unique and one of a kind. We also maintain it by replacing parts as it ages and making improvements to its design, so that it might last. How we created this miraculous form, human body, would require an entire series of ideas to explore (perhaps, a *What If,* Volume 2). That said, it did take millions of earth years to accomplish this and to reach the point where the human body is today. Over time, and through evolutionary changes, the human body continues to improve in much the same way that our human inventions and technologies do. Why? For what other purpose if not to give us the best vehicles possible to transport our spirits through one incarnation to another?

Most scientists today theorize that the human body and the human brain, as well, could not have progressed naturally to the state in which we find ourselves. They argue that not enough earth time could have elapsed for us to have evolved to this point. The question always comes down to this; did human beings have help in the evolution of physical development and intelligence? And if the speculative answer is yes, then who or what helped us? Ancient-aliens theorists would propose, that help came from outside our world, possibly from aliens. However, who are the aliens and why would they want to help us? I suspect the aliens are also our creation and another layer of existence in our Multiverse[1].

Our Capacity to Question

When we are very young, our minds are impressionable and, when we hear something thought-provoking we are not afraid to ask *why* or *how.* The frustration for adults is finding that the answers often provoke more questions and our children will continue in a cascade of questions filled with longing. Their young minds are like sponges, absorbing all that they can. Probing for answers seems to be feeding an innate desire to know and understand all that there is in the world. Sometimes adults will pass the buck, saying, "Oh, you should go ask your father (or mother)," so they can halt the questioning. Maybe, the subject matter is too uncomfortable or simply unfamiliar. But, out children do not know this, when posing such questions. They often depend upon and look forward to the adult sharing what they know. Adults usually enjoy sharing knowledge and thus is a natural human interaction.

Parents and close relatives are frontline teachers. For that reason, I always loved to ask my uncle Jack questions, because he never tired of giving answers. And, most of them sounded quite plausible and likely correct, even if they weren't. When he truly did not know the answer, he would ask, *"So what do you think, Charlee?"* That was his segue into a debate of the topic so that together we could arrive at a conclusion through logic and reasoning. Uncle Jack did not enjoy leaving questions unanswered for his fledglings. I think he secretly loved filling those gaps for himself, as well. As explorers and inventors, we receive many answers through deduction, reasoning *and* debating.

My uncle Jack had a wealth of knowledge to share and I am certain that his IQ was above average. Therefore, the answers I usually received made me secretly want to explore more, question more. Sadly, Uncle Jack made his transition quite unexpectedly and too early in this life and I truly miss his mentoring. Those thought-provoking debates might have had something to do with my own IQ rising early on. As teachers[1], our minds are kept active and running more optimally through such interactions, which is the reason so many of us enjoy sharing our knowledge *and* our opinions. We all have the capacity to pass along our knowledge in an effort to help one another. The synergies created by teacher-student relationships is evidence of our oneness and connectedness. Often, you will hear the teacher admit to learning more from their students than the other way around. When we share information, we create dynamic relationships and inspire imagination. I wonder how many of the inventions of Thomas Edison were spawned by conversations during the mentoring of Nikola Tesla.

As a student, I would often ponder our place in the Universe. In middle school, my favorite subject was science. My favorite topic was outer space, the final frontier. There was so much of the vastness of space that we could explore and, perhaps, we could understand where it all came from. Before I became hooked on Star Trek, I was fascinated with anything space related. Perhaps, it was also because, as a young lad, I grew up during the space race and watched many of the Apollo missions on television. Later, the Space Shuttle missions would continue to captivate me as a young adult. As I absorbed more, I continued to question more about our planet,

---

[1]   I use *teachers* generally to mean all of us; parents and grandparents, aunts and uncles, our siblings, preachers, neighbors, and of course teachers and professors.

solar system, and galaxy, which would help me understand how small and insignificant we were. This would ultimately lead me to question our importance and role in the Universe, as human beings, at least.

I wondered if we were just an accident, which would have me scratching my head as to how we ended up here, why, and for what purpose? I also questioned why people thought the way that they did and wondered how we all developed such different personalities. Why did we all seem so similar and yet so unique? What made up our psyches?

According to Sigmund Freud and his psychoanalytic personality theory, essentially our behaviors are composed of three fundamental psychological structures of the mind. These are the Id, Ego, and Superego. Our capacity to rationalize our immediate reality depends upon a good balance between the three.

The Id, according to Freud, deals with the self, our primal nature, our instinctive need to survive, and, to a certain degree, our attempts at instant gratification. The Id is at the root of our selfishness. When we were hunter-gatherers, our Id was responsible for keeping us alive and was in command of our actions. And now, I believe the Id has become the weakest actor of the three, taking a back seat to our Egos.

Ego deals with our conscious reality, with being conscientious, with logical thinking, the practice of delayed gratification and thoughts of personal identity. The Ego is a huge actor in the trilogy of our psyche. Albert Einstein was on to something when he said *"More the knowledge, lesser the Ego, lesser the knowledge, more the Ego.*[2] More often than not, our Egos inflate our 'self' to make up for our lack of knowledge in something. Megalomania sets in when that deflection centers on aspects of delusional greatness within ourselves in an effort to take the attention away from that which we are not knowledgeable, like a smoke-and-mirrors trick. The Ego uses this technique well. Can you think of anyone that fits this description?

When you see a person incapable of admitting that they lack knowledge in something, they will often change the subject. Usually, they are incapable of admitting that they are wrong. You will see an Egocentric individual the less they know. And it is likely that you will never see such people sharing their IQ scores with the public. Some have become masters of illusion and deception, in order to distract. They often use bait and switch in their conversations with us, as a way of keeping us from knowing the truth that they are phony or ignorant. Some are so talented at this that often we do not realize it and we buy into the con[2].

Finally, there is the almighty Superego, which dictates morality. The SuperEgo provides that underlying sense that you are doing something wrong to others, not necessarily what is wrong for you. This defines morality because it is inherent. We must agree with it for it to become a moral judgment for us. Morality transcends self, because it is no longer about what is right or wrong for you personally. Morality, something the SuperEgo is interested in, is usually centered on guilt. It is about what is right or wrong as agreed to by society. At times, this presents a psychological quandary, because you may not agree with a moral judgment about certain actions but are taught to abide by them nonetheless. This is what causes *guilt trips*. In other words, we can agree to its definition, but we may not agree with its conclusion or judgment. We feel more compelled to believe something is wrong or bad, when presented in the context of morality, because we generally accept morality as something more than just a personal preference. After all, there is safety in numbers and morality is usually agreed upon by more than one person.

For me, right from wrong is a values assessment. It is only a matter of what makes more sense and which is more beneficial, A or B. When the SuperEgo gets involved, it makes a judgment about the decision and turns right and wrong into a moral question, instead of a logical question. Again, for me, right and wrong does not have to be either good or bad. It is an assessment as to which is the more beneficial direction to take. A wrong way is not necessarily a bad way. Simply put, the wrong way is just a less beneficial option. Morality is subjective to societal whims and may or may not be logical. I think, however, logic should be devoid of any moral judgments. In any given situation, the right way should normally invoke a feeling of comfort and joy, while the wrong way may invoke a feeling of discomfort or anxiety. Remember, what's right for you may not be right for me and vice versa. You cannot use a moral judgment in a decision and expect it to align with everyone. Furthermore, we have no right to force such values upon anyone else.

---

2   *Con* is short for con artist or con man, also known as a confidence man, a person who cheats or tricks others by persuading them to believe something that is not true.

If any one of these pillars of our psyche gets too much attention within the mind, trouble may occur. Whether it be the id's self-protectionist mechanism or the Ego's self-righteous mechanism or the Superego's self-condemnation mechanism, such controlling thoughts may become problematic. I expect that psychiatry might label this a psychosis, or, at minimum, a compulsion. However, the SuperEgo gets us into trouble on its own because it helps us defend and substantiate our personal values and can trump the Id and the Ego at any time. Nevertheless, the SuperEgo is the director and, at times, the coconspirator in our personal dramas. It has a stake in many arguments, a moral obligation, perhaps. Yet, as stated earlier, a mind trap develops whenever we have trouble balancing these three main structures within our psyche. If this balance gets too far off kilter, a mental disorder may develop. If not treated, such disorders can be detrimental to the sufferer as well as to those around them.

Why is this important? Because it may be helpful to understand how our minds work in order for us to understand our place in the Universe, and perhaps further our understanding of God. And as you will soon see, it may also help explain how or why our sacred texts were written.

Finally, it is my belief that these Freudian definitions of our psyche predate human form. I speculate that they evolved the moment our thoughts began producing the world in which we found ourselves after the Big Bang. Perhaps, they are required for the mind to function sanely in the physical world. I speculate that the Ego was the first actor on stage, to help us reconcile the Big Bang of our "creation of contrast". More likely, it helped us with our perceived indiscretion. Once we adopted physical bodies, the Id came on board to help us identify with and protect our physical body and keep it alive, giving us the instinct to survive. As our bodies became more human and civilized, the SuperEgo arose to introduce morality; we required a reason for right and wrong. Of course, the order and timing of these psychic structures of the mind are simply speculation on my part. As far as I know, they could have all appeared simultaneously.

Who Are We?

When I was younger, I often wondered why I was seemingly an observer to at least two other entities in my mind, who were, at times, at odds with each other. I often had tiny arguments going on in my mind. I always assumed I was the arbiter, but what part in the conversation was I? I often had conversations in my mind about our origin as a species and I would secretly joke as to which one of these three characters of my psychic team would come up with the answer.

I feel that it is important to better understand our psychic behavior in an effort to help explain why things are the way they are and why people act the way they do. Here, I will be exploring many aspects of, at least, who and why we are and how the Ego plays an important and, sometimes troubling, role.

I will also be exploring the difference between we, the human and we, the spirit. Although most people understand there is a human world and a spiritual world, it may not be clear to some that they are very much integrated.

Source Energy

Throughout this work, you will see many references to "Source Energy". Many people throughout the world may define this as an underlying cosmic thread that we are all connected to and found throughout the Universe. I subscribe to the idea that Source Energy is where our spirits come from and is the reason why tapping into Source Energy can be so powerful. We are Creators and Source Energy is our launching point into the world of form. Source energy is a place of no place, where all of our spiritual energy originates. It is the underlying fabric of the Universe, which supported the initial creation and subsequent Big Bang. Source energy is the universal focal point and it may very well be what triggered both time and space to begin with. I also believe Source Energy is the actual birthplace for our spirits, the creation of who we are as intentions is born and is a launching point between Heaven and the physical world.

Understand that I am not a scientist and I have no scientific evidence to explain Source Energy. I can only share my understanding and conclusions through my own spiritual growth. Such conclusions deal mostly in logic and faith. I needed to make sense of both before and after the Big Bang and the conclusions you will find throughout this work are a culmination of my soul searching. Source energy is at its heart. As imperfect as the physical world is, my conclusion makes sense about how we came to be. Source energy is the bridge between the perfect and the imperfect, because once we crossed over to the world of form, we were in the land of contrast and the imperfect.

Source energy is neutral in its capacity. So, it is up to what we wish to draw from it. The successful people of the world have perfected ways to draw success and prosperity from this source, while those of less fortune are drawing difficulty and hardship. Both are using the power of intention differently. I suspect that successful people are drawing positive energy from it intentionally, while unsuccessful people are drawing negative energy unintentionally. No one of sound mind would intentionally bring adversity or hardship into their life experience. They simply do not understand the principles behind the power of attraction. This is the heart of the power of intention.

Just as it is difficult for many of us to understand certain generally accepted scientific theories of our Universe and the powers behind it, so might be the idea of Source Energy. I would liken Source Energy to a pantry containing all the ingredients ever required or imagined for our physical world, including all life and the support of it. Our successful intentions depend upon fruitful shopping out of this pantry!

Disclaimer on My Writing and Style

Religious References

What about religion? Contained herein, when speaking about religion, I may reference certain suggestions or quotations of Jesus Christ. However, I will not be exploring Christianity or any other religion in any great detail, nor do I believe that any religion is better than another. For me, all religions are set in an illusory construct, and for the most part, I view them all as well-organized social clubs. Now, there is nothing wrong with well-organized social clubs, as long as they benefit their members and cause no detriment or discrimination toward nonmembers (those on the outside). Moreover, having the benefit of something positive and inspiring does not have to have a cost to anyone else not involved in the experience, nor does it make such benefits better than anything else. This is the key to compassion and goodwill toward one another.

While I defend the right for churches to exist, I do not believe they serve the purpose that they were originally intended. Like the great Constitution written for the United States of America, certain ideas are not practical in today's world. As we evolve, so should such writings evolve. However, it is very difficult to undo such writings, as if they have been set in stone, as perhaps our most ancient texts were. I speculate that churches were once a valuable resource for the making of a stronger community. Not only were they important in helping to bring neighbors together under a common cause, they were also used to help curb civil disobedience, using tools like the Ten Commandments and similar devices. Churches were also an excellent way to convey our connection to God through Holy Scripture. Remember, most people were illiterate. Very few citizens could read or write and what better way to proselytize messages from those in power than to create a social club to help enlighten the masses from a pulpit? Clergy took the place of tribal elders around the campfire, handing down stories worth remembering, or so citizens were taught. So comes the word preach, and that person replacing the tribal elder so becomes the preacher.

Information-sharing was a challenge during a time when much of the public could barely read or write. It seems likely that, over time, those in power slanted such messages into intimidation and inflammatory rhetoric in order to have patrons comply with what they wanted to achieve, which was predominately civil obedience. I presume that some of the written texts found in many Holy Scriptures may have been fabricated to match what was being preached in our churches, synagogues, and mosques. As more of the population became literate, their message was required to match in order to maintain integrity, although not original or, in fact, not holy at all. But churches, like most successful social clubs, cannot survive without paying members. So, at some point, tithing became a mandatory way to give back for the grace received from the church. Many believe that word *tithe* comes from the number ten, and thus translates to mean *tenth*, as many references in the Bible would prove. So, to tithe meant to give one-tenth of one's income annually to the Lord our God, lest you be a heathen. And, of course, the church was the best way to convey that offering to prove you were not a heathen.

Interestingly, the greed did not stop there with some churches. As an example, the Catholic Church decided it couldn't get really wealthy without inheritance. So, the Catholic Church sanctioned that its priests could not marry and needed to be celibate, according to God, of course.

Per LiveScience[3], priestly celibacy is rooted in tradition, not Catholic dogma. Therefore, it is my contention that it was completely conjured to suit the needs of the church. Reasons vary. However, conventional wisdom holds that all assets accumulated by priests were then surrendered to the church upon death, as there would be no immediate family to inherit such assets. Over time, those assets, including not just cash but land, became the sole possessions of the Catholic Church. So, it should be no surprise how powerful the church eventually became. As we know, money is power.

There are good reasons why most people believe in some form of God or a Supreme Being, and this writing will attempt to explain, from my perspective, our relationship to God and all things of this world. I may also be able to explain how we got here and how we get home, understanding that home is not here in the physical realm. In addition, I hope to reflect on our power to attract, the power of forgiveness and finally, on the understanding that forgiveness is the ticket to our final reunion with our Creator.

In addition, I may reference God as He or Him, however, please understand that God is genderless and is more closely akin to being androgynous. For those who still picture God in human terms with long white hair and golden staff, you can thank our holy, some say sacred, texts for this imagery. Understand that we live in a physical world and need to make associations in physical terms. God, however, is not physical, this is simply a metaphor. I will explore this in more detail in the chapters that follow.

At the end of the day, we have the power to write our own ending, not always how precisely our life will end, however. Nonetheless, we do have a say in whether it will be happy or not. We can get beyond the drama of life and orchestrate an ending that will put a smile on our faces. If we will stop for a moment and release all judgments, we will find many reasons to have a happy ending.

My Writing Influences

While it is true that much of the work contained herein is the result of years of influence by notable authors and great literary works, I have tried to maintain a high level of integrity for making this my own. Where I may have copied a quote from other literary works or social media, I intentionally italicize that passage, placing it within quotes, and attempt to make it clear where it came from. Such references will be found in the endnotes. I am a firm believer in giving credit where credit is due. As such, you will find most of my literary mentors and influencers also acknowledged at the end of this writing, many of whom will always get my thanks and praise for their positive influence.

Therefore, like most people, my personal philosophy has been shaped by my exposure to a broad array of various writings and teachings. At some point, I became mature enough in my thought process to develop my own philosophies on all of the topics presented here. I have tried to use logic to weave such philosophies together into a cohesive set of ideas. I hope you will understand the tapestry I have created here. However, it is not important that you agree. It is only important that you may gain enough information to be more comfortable in your own conclusions.

My Philosophy on God

One main influence that reflects my current religious philosophy, if you can call it that, would have to be *A Course in Miracles* (ACIM)[4], as scribed by Helen Schucman and William Thetford. ACIM helped to shape my understanding of my relationship with God and bridges the gaps in sensible knowledge I found missing in the Holy Bibles. It also helped to solidify my true love for my Creator, giving me a deeper meaning in my prayer life. And, while I cannot claim absolute clarity for life itself, ACIM has added an aspect of understanding of our existence that I did not have prior to being exposed to it. It has brought peace to my personal philosophy.

As I write this, I must admit that I have been subject to, if not programmed by, a world of judgment. As such, I acknowledge that this text is infused with judgments, opinions, and even certain biases. I regret that they must be present, however, to the degree that this writing is my opinion and opinions are nothing more than judgments. All I request from you, the reader, is that you absorb this with an open mind and heart. I think if you will not take anything I say here personally and try not to judge my conclusions, it may help you with your own thought process.

So what you are about to read is not told as a story, it is simply my personal philosophy. It is a dissertation of my thoughts and opinions of our world, the Universe, God, religion, and the dream of our planet. While I may be considered Christian because of my love for the teachings of Jesus Christ, Christianity does not outline my philosophy, far from it. In fact, given my disagreements with some of what I find in both the Old and New Testaments, there may be some who will not consider me Christian at all. This is because I do not look upon the idea of Jesus Christ as a person, more likely, I view it as a concept, a values system, the 'Christ-mind' if you will. Regardless, I believe I share many of the same values of love, forgiveness, and of being non-judgmental as this Christ-mind. Therefore, it really doesn't matter what other people think I am. I hope that you may understand more about this as you continue with my dissertation here. In this work, I will raise many points in the hope of having you question your current thoughts on these subjects. If you will keep an open mind, you will be in a better position to determine if any of this resonates with you. At the very least, what I have ended up with was written with the best and purest of intentions, taking you on a journey of ideas about who we are, where we came from, and what may be our purpose here. I trust that you will enjoy the ride!

Author's Notes on Recent Updates

After some critical reviews of my first edition, this first time author was reminded how easy it is to go off on tangents, and it showed up in my writing. During my initial efforts, I found it far too easy for my Ego to wander and express thoughts and ideas that were hot topics for me personally, but that had little relevance to the overall theme of this book, which is exploring the origins of life, our relationship with God, and an understanding of the Universe at large. While I understand such tangents may confuse the reader at times, my point was to illustrate how our Egos can run amuck and divide us as humans, taking us further away from each other and our Creator, instead of bringing us all closer together.

I have also been reminded how much I may have let my Ego indulge in my writing with unflattering judgments about certain groups and certain behaviors. Since this flies in the face of my teachings, I have also attempted to expunge those judgments, unless I am trying to make a point.

In this updated edition, I have also attempted to curtail misdirection in my writing, by trying to stay focused on the primary theme. I have also deleted certain topics that did not add value to the subject matter. I trust this will help future readers with a more leisurely flow as they absorb what I have to say. Even still, minus such unabashed commentary, it is sometimes difficult for some people to digest the underlying theme that, while there is a God, He/She has no place here in our Universe because God is not of our physical world. I attempt to explain this in the following chapters in more detail, in a way that makes sense.

Thank you for your love and understanding. As always, your feedback and constructive criticism are always greatly appreciated for this first-time author.

CHAPTER 1

What if God did not create the Universe?

Most everyone who believes in God or in a Supreme Being will tell you that they often feel the presence of God in their lives. This is quite natural because, as many also believe, we are creations or children of God. What most people fail to understand is why we left God and Heaven in the first place. We will explore this in detail later, but it is important to understand that even though we physically separated from God and Heaven, it is analogous to losing a limb, once you've had it, you can never take the sense of it away, even after separating from it. This is also true for our perception of God. Our connection to the Supreme Being can never be broken. Oh, we can get angry at God for all the injustices that we encounter throughout our lives and we can even disavow God when love is taken from us. However, our anger is a mere deflection from the mortal pains we suffer here on the earth. We have no better scapegoat-in-chief than our Creator. When we see something that is not positive or is not in harmony with love, we say God damned it. When there is no one else to blame, the buck stops with Him.

It is also natural to believe that God created our Universe. Some will say it is all part of the grand design. At times, it would appear that our world, indeed, our Universe, has purpose. But, what if it was not given purpose by God? What if God had nothing to do with creating our Universe?

Anything Is Possible

My mother used to tease us kids about the what-if questions that people would pose. If someone were to say to her, "What if that idea doesn't work?" She would say, "What if frogs had wings?" And if she was given back a confused look, she would continue, "then, they wouldn't bump their asses every time they hopped!" I was sure this must have been some kind of metaphor, but I never quite understood what she meant at the time. Silly me! I would contend that if frogs had wings, they would have no need to hop at all. What if what she was trying to share with us was that we needed to stay open-minded about the possibilities of things around us, and that it is the what-if questions that keep us engaged in our human experience and in our desire to learn. Of course, she could have just been sarcastic and meant nothing by it, but I'd rather think there was an obscure lesson in that metaphor somewhere.

When I ponder the evolution of our planet in general and think of all the diverse life-forms, I always come back to "What if frogs had wings?" because I would later imagine that the power of intention created such diversity. So why don't frogs have wings? Probably because they never intended to! It is now my theory that most evolutionary changes throughout history are a result of the power of intention, as a part natural selection.[4] I believe the power of intention to succeed in life created the evolutionary changes we find today. Even to the degree that we may have intended for outside influences to help us along the way. More on that a bit latter...

No matter what the intelligence level, the drive to survive and succeed is a very powerful force. Granted, intelligence does serve to expedite the evolutionary improvement process. Why? Because the more intelligent the species, the more focus is concentrated upon that which is needed to survive. And, thus, we may find less haphazard changes in our DNA and physical makeup.

So, imagine with me, for a moment, when theropod dinosaurs were constantly under attack from the predators of the time. They must have developed a keen imagination to escape death. When their brains grew sufficiently large enough to ponder better methods by which to survive, it is likely they may have imagined the ability to escape more rapidly when under attack. Isn't it then possible they may have imagined they could even fly to escape? I think this, because when I am in a dream state where I am under attack, I run like Hell. Yet running seems insufficient to escape. So

I throw my head up with my arms straight out and back, and I imagine lifting off the ground to escape. And I do; I fly away and escape from my predators! Therefore, isn't it completely plausible that if enough intelligence had the same intentions over decades or centuries that those intentions might manifest into reality, perhaps, to the extent that certain species grew appendages more adept at jumping or even taking flight?

I have had many unanswered questions throughout my lifetime. Drastic evolution, such as that described in the above example, would be one of them. As in the case of theropods, how does a species go from running around on the ground with very little forearms to being a species that can fly?

Some of the many core questions we often ask ourselves are where did we come from, why are we here, and how did we get here? These are very pertinent questions to those hungry for knowledge.

My conclusions...

1. We came from Heaven. Since a vast number of people on planet Earth believe in God or in a Supreme Being of some kind, and most of us also believe that humans were created by that Supreme Being, then we must believe that our origination is in Heaven.
2. We are here because we wanted to experience contrast, since Heaven is devoid of contrast. We intended to have contrast, and we deliberately created it.
3. We got here the moment space-time was created out of that intention. And, with a (big) bang, here we are!

I know that the last answer will not be satisfactory for a majority of people, but how we got here is a bit more complicated to understand and requires a lot of imagination. So if you are ready for some different ideas, read on!

Where Did We Come From?

When I was around ten years old, I had an experience that blew me away and opened my mind. No, it was not LSD, I was only ten. I was lying in my bed one night, and (unbelievably) I somehow willed myself to fly, not physically, but perhaps metaphysically. It was such a strange experience, and I thought that I must've been dreaming, as my only known recollections of the strange and unfamiliar were during dream states. I remember rising out of my bed, but when I reached the roof of the house, I realized that I was free of my physical body. I sort of floated through the roof, and I knew I was flying. I was not afraid at all. I was exhilarated and enjoyed the feeling of true freedom, and so I took off and flew around the neighborhood. Before I knew it, I was flying all over Miami.

At some point, my human sensibility caught up with me as I realized I should not be able to do this. I then attempted to reconcile with my body, which I could not do. Feeling disconnected and certainly not normal, I immediately went back home. And, as quickly as I'd left, I was back in bed. I was very excited and slightly disturbed by what happened, and it took me a long time to relax and get back to sleep. I was able to execute some form of transcendental experience a few more times in the weeks to follow, but this capability was interrupted, and I would never be able to do it again. I think that this experience may have stopped after slipping up and telling my mother about it, who light heartedly said I was crazy and convinced me that I must have been dreaming. More than likely, it was my mom's negativity that changed my mind and my ability. I may never really know.

An opened mind.

What I do know is that the experience opened my mind to the idea that anything is possible, despite being told I was crazy. While I describe that experience as a dream, there was one thing that stood out and kept me thinking about it, and that was my vivid memory of South Florida's Everglades. A few years later when I was able to drive, I would visit those places by car and had a very keen sense that I had been there before. However, I also knew I had never gone there with anyone previously. It was my first experience of déjà vu, and I slowly began to remember my experience those nights at my home in North Miami when I was ten.

Since then, I have developed the belief that our world and the entire Universe may have been created out of a similar out-of-body experience and out of perhaps a primordial collective imagination to know God. So I would imagine that if enough spiritual wanting was gathered at precisely

4

the right moment in this collective daydream, a physical dimension could be created, culminating in a critical mass so huge that it produces time and space itself. I believe that a newly formed instance of time and space, in our first Heavenly intention, exploded forth with a ferocity that we now refer to as the big bang! Now, I'm not sure of the mechanics involved, but suffice it to say, it had to be monumental.

Here is another rationale. Before there was the Universe that we think we know, and before there was a physical realm of matter in this carbon-based world we live in, we children (creations) of God formed an innocent curiosity to better understand our existence with God our Creator. While we were still only just mere ideas or thoughts in what we may refer to as Heaven, we contemplated our existence. This is key. Our early ability to contemplate had enough energy to create worlds. This would give me proof of our power of intention, which I will happily explore later in chapter 5.

It may be easier for you to understand that Heaven is not a place, just as God is not a person. Neither are physical and more likely pure energy on a spiritual level. The physical Universe may have been created in that exact moment that time and space was created, in an enormous answer to understand our spiritual selves. We needed a world of form to do that and so it was made manifest out of that intention. That intention created a world of form, and thus we needed to identify with it. At that very moment of lost innocence, we were no longer conscious in Heaven. We immediately fell into a deep distraction, or sleep, in an alternate reality that we had created. It was more like our souls fell into a coma. Our human transcendental capabilities are proof that we can also step outside the confines of our physical bodies and still experience contrast, albeit in a different form. This is also evidence that we are not our bodies, that *we* are something much more extraordinary.

If one considers Heaven to be the synthesis of our ideas of paradise, then God can be considered the unity of such ideas. We were once a part of that great idea, and are actually still part of it. However, we sort of separated from God once we created time and space. If you can imagine a black hole for a moment, perhaps that is what resulted from our original intention of contrast, and then we were immediately sucked into the dimension of time and space that we had just created. Like our dreams as humans on earth, we have gone to a place that is not real. What we perceive in our dreams are nothing but partial memories of ideas or thoughts we have had. The good news is; we will eventually wake up with our full memories of our Creator restored.

How Was This Possible?

Most religions believe that we are, indeed, children of God, but many do not subscribe to the theory that God endowed us with equal powers of deliberate creation. But theologians, especially Christians, may want to look more closely at what is written in their ancient texts, and especially at what Jesus and other masters around the world were trying to convey thousands of years ago. One such biblical passage sticks out clearly, *"Very truly I tell you, whoever believes in me will do the works I have been doing, and they will do even greater things than these...."*[5] In John 14:12, Jesus was referring to the so-called miracles he could and would perform. Jesus was trying to convey to each and every one who would listen that all humans are equally endowed with the power of the miraculous. We all have the power to create, even miracles.

Many people have a hard time accepting this, just as the disciples of Jesus struggled with this concept over two thousand years ago. However, it was even worse for them because this line of thinking was considered heretical at that time. Some religions still believe to this day that we are subservient little lambs with no ability to understand that we have the power to create. It was, after all, considered blasphemy to think that we humans could all be of equal import with God the Almighty. However, Jesus knew the truth and was not afraid to share the good news, even at the risk of alienating Jewish clergy. Jesus's message was that we are one with the Father, endowed with equal powers. The real problem for Jesus back then was not that the Romans felt it was a disrespect of God. The Romans felt that their own authority might be usurped by the masses if this line of thinking were allowed to continue. Their issue with Jesus was not religious. It was more about civil obedience, with a focus on civil disobedience, and of keeping the masses in line.

For far too long, we (mankind) thought that we were weak and powerless. Otherwise, why would we allow others to rule over us? As we continued to think we were weak and subservient, we remained slaves to the wills of the rich and powerful. Keeping people in fear of God serves a similar purpose of empowering those who know the truth but are not willing to share their knowledge. People in positions of power fear they will become less and have less if they share in their resources of knowledge and wealth. Such greed promotes lies and deception. It is thought by most of the rich and powerful that there is not enough to go around. The belief in scarcity feeds the thought that only the strong (and rich and powerful) will survive. Eat or be eaten. Again, this is a huge lie. I will share more on this later in chapter 7, when I relate my thoughts on our perceived need for greed.

Jesus tried to share his understanding that all of God's creations have His same capacity to create and are equal powers endowed to us. God, our Creator, was the master cloner, if you will. Therefore, it is more than plausible that we, His children, created the known Universe. We are all co-Creators, or coconspirators, depending upon how you look at it.

So, you see, in a sense, our curiosity was an innocent conspiracy. We were in a wondrous place with our pure connection to God. So why did we need contrast at all?

Our Alternate Reality

It is not necessary to adopt the notion that our world and our existence are necessarily dreams in and of themselves, but at times, you may find it helpful to think of that possibility. Think of it this way. Our physical carbon-based world was created in an *alternate reality*. Because it is not of God or Heaven, it cannot be real and therefore must be a fabrication. True, it seems quite real for us mortals, but here is the true reality. Since this is our dream, God cannot be part of it. Oh, we can include God in this dream, and most of us do. Nevertheless, I do not know what is going on in your dream even though you may include me in it. I cannot be part of your dream and you cannot be part of my dream. God cannot be part of any of our dreams for dreams are not real— they are a fabrication within the mind. God knows we are off dreaming, just as I know when you are dreaming, but again, He cannot be part of it.

The Holy Spirit—Our Connection to God

We feel a sense of comfort by including God in our human experience, however, you must understand that it is only an illusion or distant memory of God—it is not a true connection. Many people believe we can stay connected through transcended masters. Some might call this connection as "the Holy Spirit", as does Christian doctrine with the trilogy of Father, Son, and Holy Spirit. What if the purpose of the Holy Spirit is to keep that memory as alive as possible, to keep us connected with our Creator, to keep God in our lives? Some even believe that God communicates comfort to us through the Holy Spirit, but this would mean that such Transcended Masters are simply caught up in our dream because they were, and are still, part of it. As such, they may serve as a conduit. I believe that such Masters they are willing participates in order to help us mortal beings. While I am not sure there is a direct connection, I am confident that such transcended masters, like Jesus Christ, have an enlightenment that can bring us comfort and peace in an otherwise chaotic physical world.

I believe we are born blessed and loved, and while God cannot be physically part of our human existences, God can remain steadfast in our minds through a spiritual connection. The Holy Spirit, once called the Holy Ghost, provides that indescribable connection for many of us, especially in Christianity, as does Ruh al-Qudus in Islam and Ruach HaKodesh in Judaism[6]. Many other religions can be found to hold similar connections to our creator.

The False Reality—A World of Form

Because this false reality is a world of form, we have proudly given meaning to everything in it. By giving meaning to everything we see, hear, touch, and smell, we simultaneously have given these things value. By giving them value, we set ourselves up for the possibility of that meaning or value being altered or taken away from us. This means we live in a world of fear, whether we realize it or not. By giving value to everything, we have no choice but fear that these things may be taken from us, whether that be our jobs, our homes, our health, or our relationships. For the most part, our unhappiness in life stems from the anxiety caused by this fear—a false fear that we have developed out of our attachment to the things of this world. The fear is false because the things of this world are also false. So, we create ways to cope with this fear by believing that if we try hard to be "good" and pray to God, we may keep what we value and keep the meaning for these things alive and well, and this will make us happy. I'll touch more on attachments later in chapter 6. Once we begin to place no value or meaning to the things around us, we will begin our journey back to God. This will be our ultimate challenge.

We created religions to help us keep God with us, but these are only the thought of God, not the real thing. Once we accept this world without God, we will understand why our world is a falsehood. This is why God cannot be part of it—because God cannot be part of anything false. I find it easier to think that if this world were real (for our very sanity) it is in a dimension or alternate reality outside and apart from Heaven and therefore not part of God. This will fly in the face of many that believe that God is with us and part of our reality here on earth, but again, I believe this cannot be true. Understand, this does not make me an atheist, for I wholeheartedly believe there is a God—I just do not believe that God is part of this world we find ourselves in and cannot have a direct influence in this alternate reality. God only lives in our dreams through distant memories ingrained in us, perhaps through our DNA. I will touch more on the science of our influence in Chapter 4.

Although I will delve into the world of judgments more deeply in chapter 3, I would like to touch on the subject for a moment. For those orthodox religious zealots, you might be in for a shock. Judging is not a characteristic of God—far from it. We humans created judgments the moment we created time and space. They go hand in hand, because, as I have said, we have given meaning to everything around us—and with meaning and purpose come judgments about these things. Once you understand and agree that God is not of time and space and accept that we have separated from His true realm, you will be able to agree that God can also have no judgments about our false realm. Our Creator has no vested interest here, and except for His love for us and the desire for our return, God is not part of our movie.

If I were to ask, "Do you believe that God makes mistakes or contradicts Himself?" I'm sure most of us would answer, "No! I'm fairly certain that God is perfect—you know, omni-everything. I don't think He could be contradictory because that would make him imperfect." And that observation would make that an excellent response. God is perfect because God exists in a perfect nonphysical reality, devoid of contrast.

So my simple question has always been—if God is perfect and resides in a perfect reality, how or why would He create the imperfect world we live in? Let me put it to you another way. Would you say that you believe God loves us, His children, unconditionally? Most people would respond, "Of course he loves unconditionally." All right then, here's my point. If God is perfect, and cannot contradict Himself, and loves us unconditionally, then it must be clear that God cannot be part of the world we reside in because God cannot love us unconditionally and subject us to a living Hell at the same time—again, that would be contradictory. Nor can he contradict Himself by judging us for everything mortal we do, including what some consider to be our sins! Despite what some may think, God did not put us here to test us, for wouldn't that be a hideous act, contrary to love?

God cannot love us and condemn us at the same time for that is contradictory, and I trust that we just agreed that God cannot be contradictory. He therefore cannot give us peace and war both. He cannot give us love and hate both. He cannot give us prosperity and abundance and poverty all at the same time, for to do so would demonstrate the opposite of love for us. If God were part of our world, He would never let us suffer with pain and misery, with murder and rape, with fear and war, with illness and disease! He would never let innocent children starve to death or let humans (or animals) be tortured. Since God is perfection, we must agree that all God's creations are perfect. Therefore, it is impossible for God to have created us physical beings in the first place. We are—this planet, and indeed or our entire Universe is—far from perfect. It is therefore completely illogical for God to have anything to do with this world and, therefore, He should neither be praised nor blamed for anything we perceive in it. To do so would validate Him to be a contradiction.

Having said that, I believe there is nothing wrong with praising things, including God, for the perceived good that we have in our lives. Giving thanks and praise for our abundance, and good fortune in health, relationships, and wealth is a healthy part of any prosperity consciousness[3].

---

[3]   Prosperity Consciousness is the awareness that even the smallest of positive influences are benefiting us. This lends itself to the power of positive thinking. I will expand upon this more in chapter 5.

However, these are nonetheless false impressions. They are false because they are temporary, like any value we place on such ideas about God being the source.

"But what about the world's religions?" you ask. Certainly they cannot all be wrong about their belief in God, can they? And don't most believe in our final judgment day—a judgment by God? Evangelicals who demand that there will be a judgment day may be disappointed when their time comes to pass. Judgment by God is not going to happen. The only judgment on your day of transition will be your own. If you believe you will be judged when you pass, then I am sure *you* will find plenty to judge. It is that simple. Even if God were of this world (which He is not), He would not and could not judge us.

True children of God—our true selves—are perfect just as we are. There would be no need to judge *our* behavior in *our* dreams. I mean, think about it this way—do you judge others for the dreams they may have? No. And why is that? Because, while you are aware they may be dreaming, you are not part of their perceived reality, so how can you judge it? It's the same for God. Again, He is aware that we are dreaming and is just waiting for us to awaken so we can be back with Him in the reality of our true existence. I will explore later why true forgiveness of our perceived separation from God is necessary in order to facilitate our return to Heaven and awaken from the dream that got us here in the first place. For now, just know that God loves us unconditionally and without judgment.

Why Did We Separate and Create This Place?

We separated from God in an instant when we children all had the same innocent desire to know ourselves in relation to our Creator. Think of it as our first invention. We created or invented a need, for the first time, to contrast ourselves with Him. It was an innocent idea, really, but that was the moment when we actually separated from God and felt naked, unclothed, or unprotected. It's like the fish-out-of-water analogy. The fish never knew he was any different from the water until he was no longer in it, then there was this tremendous contrast, and this was the first moment the fish knew he was no longer a part of it, that he was different, he was separate, *and* he was scared. I do not believe we intended to be separated, but you cannot have one without the other. You cannot be one with God

11

and enjoy contrast to Him at the same time. The moment we wanted to know ourselves and contrast with Him was when we created our physical realm and our perceived separation.

It truly was a massive misjudgment, and it may have been our original sin—likened, perhaps, to the garden of Eden story that the Bible claims starts our existence. I will delve more into sin later. The fact is, in order to begin our escape from this alternate reality that we call home, we must accept that we never actually left His side and that we never separated from Him in the first place. We simply need to wake up from our Heavenly daydream. Without this understanding, without accepting this responsibility, our return to God and our true homecoming cannot take place.

Some people will ask, "If He truly loves us, how could God be aware of our current circumstances and not offer to help us?" The only answer that makes sense to me is because God cannot be part of this false reality that we created. If you believe the true place for our existence should be with God, then you must believe this physical existence is a false equivalent. Just as competing poles on magnets fight each other, the true reality and the false reality will always repel in the same way. They can never join. The idea of our two realities overlapping would be as futile as trying to mix water and oil. As you know, the two just will not mix. Even if one were to try, it would not be homogenous and almost immediately separate back to the truth of each individual part—separate and distinct. This is why there is separation. The two realities cannot coexist. A world of contrast is real for us because we created it. It is not real for God because He cannot exist in a world of contrast. He/Heaven is the water and we/the Universe are the oil. Even though it was not our intention, we had no choice but to separate when we created a world of form, as the two worlds cannot comingle. We were innocent in this result, but we must now own up to it by denying it, fully and completely, for this is the only resolution to the conflict. We only need to take responsibility for creating the conflict, as innocent as it may have been, but we must forgive ourselves for creating it at the same time. True forgiveness is our only responsibility. You must understand that we cannot escape the indiscretion that we created if we remain in guilt of it. The indiscretion, or separation, must be completely forgiven. This requires true love for ourselves as children of God. This was the message given to us by Jesus Christ himself, more than two thousand years ago, with his parable of the Prodigal Son. We only need to believe that God loves us unconditionally, and without fear of judgment. Such is the truth of this biblical parable.

CHAPTER 2

What if we created the Universe by dreaming it?

As my all-time hero Carl Sagan[7] is quoted as saying, *"We are made of starstuff."* That's a hint that we must look outside our immediate domicile on earth to find the answer. Many of our advances today stem from mad science or crazy fiction that, given time, had a chance to be proven reality or eventual technology. People who think outside the box actively participate in being Creators and making things happen because they think they can. Remember—in a dream, anything is possible!

I, like so many of us, have struggled with the question "Where did we come from?" Surely, we are more than just hatched fertilized human eggs, aren't we? The problem humans have is thinking beyond questions such as, "Which came first, the chicken or the egg?" It is very difficult for the human mind to grasp anything microscopic or macroscopic without the actual tools to make evidence of it, and yet even with tools as evidence, it is difficult to conceive that which is not within our perspective.

The common man might admit to his brain hurting when trying to fathom the sheer size of our known Universe, for example, because to most of us, the vastness of the Universe is simply inconceivable. So there is a certain point at which our brain stops trying to rationalize and make sense of it. Why? Because it is of relatively useless value in our daily lives—therefore, it does not need to be part of our understanding and our everyday perspective in order to survive. Only those who have made it a career to understand the vastness of the Universe can develop and use the tools necessary to comprehend it, but most of us find little need to include this in our perspective. We are happy little frogs in the slowly boiling pot, comfortable with what we know at any particular moment, until … well, you know what happens. For now, we just accept that the Universe is very large.

We Wondered, Then Wandered

So there we were, happy and content and one with our loving Mother/ Father God. We began to wonder about contrast and wandered outside our confines of thought in Heaven. We were literally out of our minds. Somehow, we got lost in that dream, and ever since, like some *Twilight Zone* movie, we have been trying to find our way back to God and out of this nightmare.

In trying to tackle what transpired after our initial indiscretion, our focus might be—what is our place in the Universe? What is our purpose or destiny? What is the purpose of Ego, and why does Ego drown out the innate love that God endowed us with? Just as in science, we have to be prepared for more questions than answers as we probe to find out where we came from and why we are here. Do not be too surprised if you begin questioning your own ideas as you explore the what-ifs of how we came to be.

Let There Be Light

Before there was a beginning,

God was all there was, and it was good. Out of pure love sparked desire—a desire to create more and to share in it. And thus, God multiplied that love and created us spirits. As you may discover, *A Course in Miracles* will label this creation (us) as the Christ Mind. This capacity to create has also been endowed in us. After all, according to the Bible, we are children of God, created in His likeness.

Many newer (more accurate) theories of Heaven would have us view the place where God resides as in a dimension devoid of time and space, not containing a world of form as we know it. This is easy to understand. Some would even go further and say it is also devoid of energy, defining energy as a construct of both time and space in a physical carbon-based world of form that makes up our known Universe. If we accepted this, Heaven would certainly be a difficult world to understand given our need to contrast it—which is our human nature. This is how humans have expanded knowledge, because we have developed a keen ability to compare and measure, and we've developed technology in order to prove and substantiate it. These abilities are what have given rise to the sciences of biology, chemistry, mathematics, cosmology, and even astronomy.

Getting Back to Heaven

The benevolence of God was to share His goodness, and out of His love was created a consciousness of individual thoughts in which to share and multiply that love. At some point, there began an expansion of other ideas related to that pure love, such as joy and contentment, which eventually gave rise to a consciousness of those ideas or thoughts. Finally was born the thought of awareness itself—an awareness that we might be part of something bigger, all experiencing the same thing, sharing the same. This may have been the precursor to the idea of self, which must have been somewhat confusing in a world of nothing, no form. After all, we were merely ideas of love, born from God. But as that love expanded, so did our awareness.

This true awareness—of something outside ourselves—eventually led to a desire to know ourselves *and* each other and to explore this new consciousness. Contrast was needed. But the only way to do that was, again, outside us. So how did we do that? *We began to imagine and dream!*

Pure Innocence

In our innocence to explore and play with ideas about our existence in God's realm, we began to dream. In those dreams, we found a collective of other forms of consciousness. We found ideas in expression from many of our Heavenly siblings. And out of that sparked the thought that there was something else—but we had nothing to compare that thought to. From that very moment, we became aware of something in world of nothing. We began to question our consciousness. Before that moment of such profound awareness, we were like babies in our mother's womb—content in our oneness with God, enveloped in pure love. Since there is no such thing as time and space in Heaven, pure love completely occupied our existence, and we were content with God. We were surrounded in peace and tranquility. So what happened?

Relativity

Like most children, we eventually began to have questions about our reality, yet the answers seemed incomplete for some reason. Understand that in a formless world, Heaven is not a place, and God is not a person. We have no corporal bodies. We are formless. At some point, we began to have individual thoughts even though we were part of a larger mind-set. This must have caused a rip in what was previously a very cohesive existence. It's not that we began questioning our Father's wisdom or the perceived answers when we developed questions, but rather, like the motives of scientists today, we only sought to corroborate His answers by being able to compare ideas. We were innocent in our curiosity, but we wanted some form of relativity. Yet how could we do that in a world without contrast?

Again, since Heaven is formless, we had to devise a way to experience ourselves in very inventive ways. We had thoughts, but we did not have form, and without form there is nothing to contrast against. So, we birthed a desire to compare, and we began to dream what that might look like. This was the beginning of our idea of separation from God. We went off somewhere to dream. Once we set out to play, we left His kingdom, even if only for a split second in a world of no time. We did it in a dream!

It all happened as enough ideas and thoughts, before we were actual beings, took hold with a common desire to have answers to our primitive questions. At that moment, a focal point was set, and a convergence of this same consciousness created a space-time continuum (now I sound like Doc in *Back to the Future*). This is where things got dicey, because, at that moment, we immediately transferred our thoughts into this new dimension as we identified in it. Our thoughts were now fully engulfed in the dream, and in that dream we began to get the contrast we desired, all from just one common idea. Contrast was the only way that we could experience ourselves, and now *we could compare!* The collective dream gave a "place" for our convergence of thoughts and relativity was born.

Thought Bubble

Think of the Universe as a thought bubble. All matter making up the Universe resides inside this bubble, but it did not start out that way. Originally, this thought bubble resided in a realm of matter-less energy, containing no-thing. At some point, such thoughts were transformed and burst into the world of matter that we know, yet it was still in a bubble. So, if you were to actually attempt to reach the edge of our Universe of matter (our bubble), setting out in a straight line, you would end up back where you started at the inside of the bubble. You would have no idea when you'd actually reached the outer edge of the bubble, as it would simply continue in a complete circle around its inner circumference. It would be analogous—albeit the complete opposite—to flying around the earth in a straight line, around its outer circumference, eventually circling back where you began.

I know that's a lot to imagine. Bear with me for a moment, and open up your imagination even further. The bubble started out very small, as just one thought of what contrast would be like. Other thoughts of the same type coalesced, just like soap bubbles coming together in your kitchen sink, colliding and forming an even larger bubble. One thought bubble probably did not have a huge impact on the world of thought. As a single thought, it would remain mostly an idle idea. But when enough thoughts—all of wanting the same thing—built upon each other, enough energy was created by the collision of ideas to start the expansion of that thought bubble, trigger the creation of matter, and ultimately cause the expansion of our known Universe inside that thought bubble.

I know, that's a bit much to grasp, right? But here's my rationale:

I liken this thought processing to the energy (heat) put out by our computers. At idle, processing very little information, the computer is still active because the CPU is waiting to process something. While the computer is idle, it is generally running very cool and quiet. But when the computer starts processing information, running various tasks, loading up the CPU with lots of activity, heat is produced. As the CPU approaches 100 percent utilization, the microprocessors heat up very quickly because—even at the microscopic level—information (atoms) are moving all around the computer at atomic speeds, from input devices collecting and transferring the data to the CPU, to the CPU computing what to do with that information, to the output devices which store that processed data. The more information being processed, the more atoms are being moved around using energy and creating heat in the exchange. All this activity creates heat because this internal energy (the atoms) are moving at very rapid speeds, albeit microscopic. It's like taking a coat hanger and bending it back and forth. Bending it very slowly usually doesn't produce much change, but start bending it back and forth very quickly, and the atoms become more excited. This atomic excitement creates heat and—if enough atoms are excited at the same point of attraction—the metal in the hanger softens, changing composition, and can easily break in half. For the same reason, components on the computer motherboard can get so hot that they could literally burn you if you were to touch them. In the early days of computers, when higher electric voltage was needed to operate solid-state computer components, enormous efforts were required to counter all the heat created by this processing. Heat sinks, some water cooled, some nitrogen cooled (and later A/C air cooled), were introduced to pull the heat away from delicate semi-conductors used in computer motherboard in order to keep cool enough to work properly. I believe the term meltdown probably came out of the computer industry as early computer components literally fried in the absence of effective heat sinks to pull away the tremendous heat created by their excited atoms.

I experienced this firsthand when a laptop of mine must have had a cooling fan or heat sink fail. I had it, as one might guess, sitting on my lap while I was researching something on the Internet. Like the frog in the slowly boiling kettle, I did not realize how hot it had gotten until it was almost an emergency. I threw the PC off my lap and remember yelling, "Ouch!" It literally scorched my leg and looked, for hours, as though I had been sunburned. Although the CPU could not have been utilized at 100 percent, there was plenty of data being moved from the Internet to my screen and into my digital notes. The problem was that the heat created by this activity was not being pulled off the motherboard, which allowed the machine to build up more and more heat—to the point that the laptop screen began to quiver and get distorted.

Why is this relevant?

At some point, enough thoughts in our thought bubble began processing what-if questions. As you may know, oftentimes these questions spark even more questions. This buildup of thoughts and questions in our original thought bubble began multiplying, and similar to the heat that builds up in our computer processors, eventually there was a change in this pre-atomic composition. I envision an explosion created what we now understand as our Universe of matter. I believe physicists might say that a critical mass had occurred. Similar to the computer processor being overloaded, or overheated, with the processing of data, the Universe began to take form, and contrast was immediately born. Perhaps a natural response, in this enormous event, was to expand in order to help calm down and cool the chaos being created. But contrast needs an observer, and I believe we were already present, albeit without form, to begin this process.

So it is my idea that we sprang forth out of the thought bubble and eventually found a way to hijack the matter that was also created. Since that time, we (and all in our Universe of matter) have been seeking to cool down by expanding, forming a natural heat sink. And thus, we keep multiplying and expanding. Where this will lead, no one knows for sure. Even scientists and astrophysicists cannot agree. Some say the Universe will continue to expand, Ad infinitum. Some say it will eventually collapse in on itself, imploding to its eventual demise. While others believe there will be a continuous cycle of expansion and collapse, analogous to our lungs taking in air eventually requiring exhalation and repeating the process in a natural balance.

The Big Bang of Thought

Our what-if thoughts must have been what sparked the first appearance of time itself. In a place of "no things", time is not necessary. But in a world of physicality, now there are "things" involved in our awareness, and, time is required for measuring everything of matter. We cannot exist in this physical dimension without time. It is impossible to have contrast without time, so the two go hand in hand. Einstein wrote much on this subject in his theories of relativity. Contrast depends upon relativity, so it would make sense that we intended all the ingredients that make up relativity in these very first instances of time-space and motion, and light was born from this convergence of energy and radiation.

So, there we were, in the beginnings of another world, still without form yet in a world of space and time, a new world of form where contrast was originally created. At that moment, we realized that we were not in Kansas anymore. We were no longer in Heaven. We had separated from God! Great Scott, what had we done? We'd dreamt up a world of contrast and we were living the dream now, all thanks to a new dimension of time and space that we had created. Simultaneously—once we realized what we had created—we must have had our first feelings of being alone and of being cold and scared. While dreaming the dream to experience ourselves, in all our pondering, we'd accidentally created time and space. God had enabled us with all the powers to create, all we had to do was ask, and it was given.

While we were still only thoughts, we were now thoughts in a world of form, and we began to identify with objects in it. Our first emotion out of this contrast must have been fear—fear that we must have done something wrong, that we were completely out of our safety zone, that we were completely out of our league. We were innocent, but like our Father in Heaven, we were Creators now. Our thought bubble had erupted to create an alternate reality of form in a new world of time-space. This must have felt like an enormous burden—another new emotion out of contrast.

An alternate reality – really?

Certainly the above explanation of the big bang could be explained as easily as any other theory for it, right? Maybe not. I mean, try and explain string theory, for example. It's a great theory, but it cannot be explained with the data from our known Universe, because the theory depends upon a multiverse that lies beyond our senses and our current technology. But think about that for one moment. If you accept the possibility that we created our known Universe, who's to say that other unknown Universes were not also simultaneously created, and that they, perhaps, may even overlap in some strange way in this fog of a multi-dream. Similar to our cells dividing during reproduction, perhaps our original thought bubble acted to create the ingredients needed for separate –multiple- Universes. Making matters even more interesting is the idea by some that our spirits can pop in an out of any of these multi-verses at any time, giving rise to the doppelgänger concept and creating feelings of déjà vu, and, perhaps, even explaining where our genius originates. And perhaps, this could also help explain the belief, by some, in elusive "extra-terrestrials" and how they might pop in and out of our reality.

Of course, another theory for déjà vu could also come from those who believe that our spirits can incarnate in multiple life forms in this world, not just one. This gives an answer as to there being more and more hosts available as we expand and multiply. It's an interesting theory; what if, it were true?

If these ideas create even more questions for you, then you are one step closer to understanding how compounding ideas in such thought bubbles could have resulted in the critical mass needed to create Universes in the first place! Yet, string theory, like any other theory, can only survive if the theory is widely accepted as plausible or until a better, more widely accepted theory surfaces to trump it and take its place. And, of course, once a theory is proven, it is no longer a theory and becomes fact—but this almost always leads to more questions and more new theories spawned to substantiate them.

To me, science is not much different than religion, to the degree that one has to rely on faith in both much of the time. If a scientific theory is published, and if it becomes plausible, enough people will have to have faith that it is true until otherwise proven false. Such faith gives rise to the creation of technology in order to substantiate the theory. The biggest difference is that faith in religion is more analogous to big government. Even when aspects of government are proven wrong, it may simply be ignored or take an act of Congress to change people's minds about it. And one could argue that religion has existed and been accepted a lot longer than science has. So the belief structure in religion is more established and entrenched in our minds. Even so, both religion and science often still use the hypothetico-deductive method of reasoning, which basically holds that the lack of evidence proving a subject is false makes the subject automatically true. However, sometimes a theory cannot be incontrovertible, as Einstein meant when he said, *"No amount of experimentation can ever prove me right. A single experiment can prove me wrong."*[8]

The problem in trying to answer the questions that arise from the big bang theory is that no matter how smart we get or how advanced our technology becomes, we may be chasing our own proverbial tails. This illusive dream that we created does not have an answer because before space and time there was, in fact, no things, and nothing by its very nature has no contrast—therefore, it has no explanation since there is nothing to measure. It's just a thought or idea. To have something, you need space. To measure things, you need time and space. And while I cannot claim to understand the theory of relativity, I do get the relative importance of time in our world. It is at the center of everything we know.

This brings us back to God as the underlying force of the nothingness out of which we came. And yet, later in history, man would write the first book—the Holy Bible—and would ascribe our amazing creation to God, when God supposedly said, *"Let there be light."* If God were a witness to our creation, our dream, He might have remarked that very profound observation. Indeed, let there be light, for our newly formed world of contrast very much required and depended upon it!

CHAPTER 3

What if our need to judge was only meant for survival?

I believe the first time I realized that I had lost my innocence I was probably only eight years of age. I was staying the weekend at my grandparent's house. Saturday morning, my grandfather took me for a ride to visit a friend, the pastor of a local Methodist church. There, I met his son—a nice kid named Dickie. We fooled around out in their backyard, playing with his toy soldiers and tin car toys, while my grandfather and the pastor were in the house tending to some other business. Gramps had a prominent standing with the Masons, and I think he was chatting with the pastor about the lodge or some other business.

After a while, I began to get bored. Dickie pulled out a cool pocketknife. It looked brand-new, and I could not take my eyes off it. The knife seemed to be of no importance to Dickie, as he left it laying on the patio along with all his other toys. My gramps and the pastor came out to the patio to conclude their discussion. When we were getting ready to leave, I conveniently picked up the knife and put it in my pocket without anyone seeing. At that moment, I lost my innocence because I knew that I was taking something that did not belong to me. I was stealing Dickie's knife. Something inside me convinced me that it was okay, even though I knew it was wrong. After spending a couple hours with the kid, I reasoned that he had more than he really needed, as he seemed to hardly have time to play with all the toys he had. Actually, he seemed like a rich little kid to me and, in retrospect, I believe this may have been my first judgment—a judgment to justify my thievery. While my SuperEgo tried to reason that taking his knife was wrong, my Ego overruled that and had me convinced he would never miss it, and that I needed it more than he did. Later that afternoon, I heard the telephone ring. I heard my grandfather speaking with someone and eventually realized it was the pastor. Afterward, Gramps came to me and asked me if I took the knife from Dickie. I was so embarrassed, I immediately made up a lie and said that he'd given it to me. Gramps argued that it was not a gift and that I had stolen it, and I was ordered to give it back. Gramps drove us back to their house, and—in shame—I was forced to hand the knife back over to Dickie. As I suspected, he couldn't have cared less, and in fact said, "No, you can keep it!" Of course, that was not going to happen. Gramps was furious, ashamed, and embarrassed at what I had done.

I never forgot that day because of the shame and pain that I caused—all self-inflicted, of course. I had stolen, and I had judged someone in order to justify the offense in my mind. I had labeled Dickie a rich little kid as another way to justify taking something that did not belong to me. I had lied in order to cover up my shame. In an instant, all the fun of the day was erased, and I felt that my reputation with my grandfather was forever tarnished. I cannot recall if I was actually punished, but seeing the disappointment in Gramp's eyes was more punishment than a month of chores and a belt to my bottom. I believe that I punished myself with self-judgment for a long time thereafter, and it seems that, even to this day, I am reminded of my fault. As it turned out, my grandfather would forgive me and the incident was never spoken of again. I suppose his love for me could not sustain any negative judgment of me. It was an early lesson of love and forgiveness but it was also a lesson about the negative consequences of being judgmental. In retrospect, I can see how the Ego can affect us in negative ways. Even in a little boy, Ego can supplant our judgment of self-protection to one inducing greed.

An Ego Is Born

So there we were, in a new world of thought. When we first realized that we had done something monumental in Heaven as new Creators, we lost our innocence. As the subsequent drama unfolded after the big bang, it must have felt like Adam and Eve's need to be clothed. Perhaps we were ashamed. We certainly must have been afraid. Maybe that is where the biblical story came from. Moreover, out of that fear was born the Ego, for in questioning what we had done, we forced the need for an answer, and Ego stepped in to answer what had occurred.

Even though we had not yet created life-forms in which to adopt the senses needed to experience this new place of time and space, we did establish a world in which contrast could be perceived. Consequently we had gotten a hitchhiker in the process—*self-awareness*, otherwise known as an Ego. Our identity with "self" had created a monster from the very beginning because now we were getting answers that we had to reason with. What if our world of matter was created from such reasoning, kind of like pieces to a jigsaw puzzle coming together to form a picture?

Remember the old saying, "Be careful what you wish for"? We wanted contrast, and we got it, but consequently the Ego became part of the package. Freud would also include the Id and Superego[8]. Ego is an offshoot of contrast and pops up at every turn in our lives. It justifies our existence in this world of contrast and is the reason we must name things with labels and with judgments about them. It is also the reason we have anxiety about things we judge, creating guilt and fear, out of which was born the SuperEgo and our Id. Fear, which is the antithesis of love, was born out of the contrast we created. We fear that which we do not understand but our ID also uses fear to protect us.

Fast-forward to Human Beings

After we created and adopted life-forms to experience the contrast we had created, Ego was responsible for our first need to label things in our human development. Our primal need to judge things in our environment was born out of our need to survive. Early on, we judged the distance from a cliff to the ground in order to determine if a fall or jump was survivable. We judged whether another creature was dangerous and could possibly harm us—eat or be eaten was a matter of judgment in many cases. Judgments were responsible for fight-or-flight responses, and they were always about our very survival. The better we became at accurately judging threats, the better our chances for survival. In a sense, judging things was purely a binary decision-making process—you believed more in A or B, or something was either true or false. Some would argue that it was our early judgment of our environment that helped us learn logic.

Our Need for Labels

Initially, the Ego was a helpful contributor in our agreement to create contrast. Ego was part of self-preservation before the Id found its purpose. We now had a physical body, and we needed protection. Thus, Ego helped us by creating labels for things so that we could associate in the world of form. This ultimately led to the need for a vocabulary and language. We created words for everything—horse, tree, fire, sky. Then Ego convinced us that we should classify them as well—*brown* horse, *tall* tree, *hot* fire, *dark* sky. This became very important during communication because if I wanted you to bring me a horse, which horse would it be that I wanted? You might bring me the *white* horse, when I'd really wanted the *brown* horse because he was faster during a hunt. Later in human development, we would get even more descriptive by giving animate objects proper names, because there could be many different brown horses. So once again, which brown horse did I really want? Our society or group would agree to these names for future ease of reference, so one could say, "Bring me Lightning Chaser," or, "Sky Dancer," both being brown horses—but with a difference now. In a world of contrast, we needed to be specific in order to effectively communicate and get what we wanted.

Once we had labels and classifications for things, we were all-powerful, because we then had dominion over these things, and we had clarity and purpose for them. So our Egos grew. But we didn't stop there. We decided it was also necessary to group things, so we added judgments to the labels, and this is where we really went *wrong* (oops, there's another judgment)!

When Ego convinced us to give our opinion on the labels we gave things, such as *good* horse, *ugly* tree, *bad* fire, *beautiful* sky, we added a whole new dimension to our world of contrast. I must make a distinction here between our ability to classify and our need to judge things, because one could argue they are both judgments. However, classifications are not usually subject to one's opinion, because they are agreed upon by a consensus of those people using them, while judgments are subject to one's unique interpretation and may stand alone. But Ego does not care if you stand alone in your judgment of a thing, because if you require assignment using a label for a thing then it must be worthy and in fact correct— all other's opinions be damned. And do not be fooled by appearances, either—a dove, the symbol of peace and unity, is nothing more than a white pigeon. Shouldn't we see the irony in the labeling of pigeons as ugly and dirty little creatures, while the same creature—the dove—is labeled as beautiful and pure?

Classifications are more benign, as they tend to take on simple labels, and they are usually agreed upon to aid in our description. Which horse? The *white* horse. Judgments, on the other hand, are subject to our opinions, and those can be damaging, misleading, and even threatening.

Right and Wrong: Our Need to Judge

From the moment we are born into physical bodies, we are taught to label things. Everything must have a name. Ego gives us the need to label things for many reasons. We are quickly taught things like mother, father, sister, brother, apple, orange, etc. Everything must have a label, for this is how we learned to associate with the things around us. Accurate association of things in our environment not only made us smart, it could save our lives.

Again, we did not stop with mere labeling. Early on in our development, we were programmed by our parents, siblings, friends, teachers, and preachers not to simply associate with things, but to *judge* them, and our SuperEgo was quick to help us with that. So our early ideas about the world we live in quickly became more than simple associations. They became rather complex judgments about our world. For example, good/bad, pretty/ugly—everything in life is a judgment, not just a simple association. A woman by the name of Byron Katie refers to this human characteristic in her insightful book called *Loving What Is*, where she tells us that this is, in fact, "our job on the planet. We judge. This is what we do. When we say, *it's raining*, that's a judgment. *the sky is blue*, that's a judgment!". While Ms. Katie is correct in the broader sense, I make the distinction that those examples are, in fact, personalized characteristics, not necessarily judgments—but one could argue that any distinction between Ms. Katie's viewpoint and my own about categorizing with associations is also a judgment. So, to each his/her own.

Associations are generally harmless, usually benign labels that are accepted by more than one person in order to make it easier to relate with one another and function more easily in society. Judgments, on the other hand, have the potential to be harmful in nature and are more than just simple associations.

Judgments (good/bad, pretty/ugly, lawful/criminal, honest/liar, etc.) are oftentimes dangerous inflections of one's personal opinions and usually meant to stir the opinions of others. They may also be slanderous and cast doubt or fear about the subject matter. In some cases, they can be used as character assassinations. Some may even go so far as to paint a picture of evil with them. An example would be the judgment calls of radical Islamic jihadists. Islamic jihadists use such judgments about Americans to incite violence and carry out their cause. The phrase *America is the great Satan* is an example of a judgment so powerful that even some conservative Muslims may eventually buy into it and be called to arms. But when asked, "Who is the great Satan?" it most often comes down to a scant few in the government who hold the power to make policies and edicts that often times violate the will and the rights of others, sometimes others in a sovereign country. The irony is that if you were to ask the American people, some would not agree that the American government represents them or their views, so annihilation of all American people for their government's policies makes about as much sense as the annihilation of all Muslims for the policies and edicts of Islamic jihadists. Both groups have been hijacked by the judgments of a few.

There is indeed power in the spoken word, and the speeches of Adolf Hitler in the early twentieth century are another good example. Hitler was able to incite two World Wars with his words. Mostly, Hitler communicated his ideas through instilling fear in the citizens of Germany. Using judgments and instilling fear are the easiest ways to convince people that your analysis and opinions are correct because fear plants the seeds of doubt which often cloud logical thinking. And fear instills the "better be safe than sorry" premise in the decision making process of most humans. Judgments can lead to confusion or worse. They can actually lead to war.

Is it really necessary to call the tree *ugly* in order to identify it, or can we be satisfied to say it is the shorter tree nearest the river? Similarly, is it necessary to call a fire *bad*? It may be bad to you because you got burned by a fire previously, but it may be good to me because my food tastes better heated by a fire. So for me, the fire is good. Likewise, forest fires appear bad or destructive, but to many ecologists they appear to be a natural occurrence in our world and actually help to clear out undergrowth of the forest, helping to make it actually thrive.

Here is my point—the fire is neither good nor bad. It is just a fire. As you can see, judgments give rise to arguments about them, and arguments can lead to hostility and war, because you are either in agreement with the judgment or not. Most people can agree on a classification of a thing.

What's in a Word?

In my opinion, when a word is used as a judgment it is normally not for good (*oops, I just made another judgment*). Even when used in a complimentary way, it can unintentionally be perceived as a put-down. Imagine, you are talking to Sharon and Debbie walks in the room. You make a comment. "Gosh, Debbie sure is pretty today."

The mere fact that you have not said the same to Sharon may leave her feeling ugly. So, even seemingly benign compliments can have a negative effect on people without your realizing it. But we do it all the time. I think we would be better off if we could judge less and love more, for love and respect are the highest form of compliments there are. And one does not have to speak to show love. Love is more about our actions, not our words. It's how you show compassion for others that matters most.

Now, there is another distinction worth noting. There are some judgments or values given to things that can be useful as an association when it is necessary to define a helpful characteristic, such as in weights and measures. If you say *the suitcase is too heavy to carry*, that's a judgment that can be helpful and not used against another. Such nonpersonal value judgments are simply an extended association and not really a judgment. It is okay to label things in order to be helpful. *The stove is hot* is a helpful judgment about the stove that I might make in order to spare someone pain from getting burned.

Why do I make these distinctions? Because judgments often spark debate, which can lead to arguments, fights, and even wars. I believe this is the reason Jesus is quoted as saying, *"Judge not."* And while that passage goes on to say, *"That ye be not judged,"* I do not believe that he meant it to mean *go ahead and dish it out as long as you can take it in return*. No, Jesus was trying to give a point of reference as to why we should not judge things. If you can admit to how hurtful or upsetting it is to have it done to you, then there is certainly merit for not doing it to others.

Sinning

Jesus is also quoted as saying, "*He that is without sin among you, let him first cast a stone...*[10]" Now, I would like to clarify what context the judgment word *sin* was used in. For me, *sin* simply means fault. Actually, it is thought that the word sin is an age-old Aramaic archery term, meaning *to miss the mark*. So, two thousand years ago, you were a sinner for just about anything if your actions were held up in a court of public opinion. I like the distinction made in many writings which refer to a very old definition of sin. The opinion of one such writing takes interpretation even further by saying,

So what IS sin?

SIN actually came from an Aramic Language, it's the term Jesus used, translating the word "Hamartia" which is a Classic Greek Word... And here's the funny thing, you know where Jesus used the term? IN ARCHERY...

YES! In Archery!

Sin, along with EVIL, are archery terms... Sin meaning "TO MISS THE MARK" and Evil meaning "THE UNINTENTIONAL MARK"... And yes, JESUS used these terms as a positive feedback...

How did Jesus use these terms?

Since that SIN means MISSED THE MARK, it was meant to mean you have worked on something that has MISLEADING INFORMATION... Somehow, when your conscience become aware of it, YOU WILL HAVE THE OPTION TO CORRECT IT... That's what Jesus meant!... When you actually commit a "SIN", you will have the choice to correct it... And EVIL is just the MARK of that MISLEAD ACTION...

That's what SIN really means...[11]

So what does this mean? Today's usage of the word *sin* is used to describe something bad, wrong, or evil. But understand that words like *bad* and *sin* are judgment words and subject to the perception of the person using those words. Somewhere along our physical evolution (and certainly with Ego's help), we developed the capacity to judge instead of just associate. We inflect our individual opinions on just about everything. So we go from mother/father associations to judgments like good/bad and pretty/ugly. I believe this is the job of our Egos, which take over sense and sensibility. So why does the Ego like to judge others? Because it can! Perhaps its only job is to have us question our sense and sensibility. But we have gotten lazy and allowed our Egos to run amuck.

Another definition according to ACIM is this,

> *Sin is defined as "lack of love" (Text, p. 11). Since love is all there is, sin in the sight of the Holy Spirit is a mistake to be corrected, rather than an evil to be punished. Our sense of inadequacy, weakness, and incompletion comes from the strong investment in the "scarcity principle" that governs the whole world of illusions. From that point of view, we seek in others what we feel is wanting in ourselves. We "love" another in order to get something ourselves. That, in fact, is what passes for love in the dream world. There can be no greater mistake than that, for love is incapable of asking for anything.*[12]

I believe that Sin and sinning are topics introduced in religious texts in order to reign in the perversions of mankind. They are always used in judgments of right and wrong. They are condemning words. They are very much subject to the author's agenda, and so I do not personally adhere to many of the notions presented about our sins in ancient texts, because I do not agree that God judges our behavior. Man judges our behavior. The use of the word *sin* in our ancient texts imposes judgment upon us, therefore, any such references are out of integrity with our Creator. The wisdom of Jesus Christ is enough for me to discount all references to sin. We all have an opportunity to correct times when we have missed the mark, when we have made mistakes, and the only judgments about these indiscretions should be used in the opportunities for correcting them.

Consider sin as the idea of getting off course in your life. The correcting of our sins is merely a course correction. The most important takeaway about sin is that it should remain a personal observation and a personal decision to correct. Any such observations from anyone else about you is not about you, it is about the person making the observation. Humans love to project their observations about their own indiscretions outward, onto someone else. You know this. And sometimes, they are projecting someone else's indiscretion onto you. It is an unfair three-way because the person in question is usually not around to defend themselves. At times, it is merely a deflection because (my theory is) the more you can show the faults of others, the less the spotlight is on you. Can you think of anyone who does this? It is almost always a third-party deflection because people do not have the courage to speak directly with the person they are accusing. Therefore, it is a clear demonstration that the accusation—or sin—is not about you. It is about the accuser.

In conclusion, sin is an Egotistical label for calling out someone in a negative light. Since we all have our faults—or sin—in varying degrees, we should not cast the first stone at anyone (i.e. accuse) because that would make us hypocrites. I believe this is what Jesus meant to share with us. What I say is—clean up your own backyard before asking others to clean theirs. Even then, the best advice I can give, my friends, is to keep your criticisms to yourself!

When Ego Thrives

It is quite amazing to see the Ego in action, and one cannot think about the Ego without visualizing the 2016 GOP presidential nominee. For simplicity here on out, I will refer to him as *the 2016 GOP nominee*. Throughout the years, this man has let his Ego rule most of his decisions—and very successfully, it would seem. This man has used his Ego to become a master manipulator, and he is also a master at changing the focus of topics by calling people liars. When anyone contradicts what he says or does, he brands him or her a liar. When journalists and other candidates portray his actions or speeches in a negative light, he attempts to mock, belittle, and defame them. This is the sign of a bully, and an unchecked Ego is to blame. When organizations, such as our free press, try to call him out on his rants, he says they are being unfair to him. He then adopts a strategy of defaming them, calling them 'Fake News'. His Ego helps create fictitious conspiracy theories to support his accusations. In fact, seeing his actions in recent years would indicate that anyone who does not support him is surely being unfair to him, and he will often spout, "*These are not good people.*" So you are either with him or against him. There is no in between. But watch out! If you are not for him, you might be labeled bad, evil, or corrupt. He dribbles disparaging words like a basketball, always holding on to this form of negativity, never moving on, never passing the ball. He is a malevolence hoarder.

I mentioned earlier of the keen ability for humans to use labels and the spoken word as weapons. It seems that the 2016 GOP nominee has made a fortune capitalizing on his spoken words, and he uses his success as ammunition for speaking out. He also speaks poorly about subjects to bolster his own standing. His entire 2016 presidential campaign was based upon showing how wrong people were and how bad things were in order for him to look better. You could hardly get through one of his speeches without hearing him blaming someone for something, calling out a "*disaster*" about something, or constantly sighting systems being rigged as the reason he wasn't getting ahead.

As the famous W.C Fields is quoted as saying, "If you can't dazzle them with brilliance, baffle them with bullshit!"[13] The 2016 GOP nominee will often throw you a curveball with his litany of superlatives and other adjectives, like *tremendous, fantastic, super,* or *outrageous,* and to close the deal with you he will throw in, *believe me.* It is a mind game, and he has learned it very well. And let's not forget "*I'm hearing this or that ...*" or "*A lot of people are saying ...*" These are all remarks that add to his narcissistic personality. He loves to plant seeds of doubt and waters them with repetition. And he covers himself with many just-in-case words like *probably, maybe, likely,* and let's not forget "*Just so you understand ...*" and "*That I can tell you.*" He is a master at not being definite about anything except for the lies he spews. He is a master at selling you his thoughts with hyperbole, and some would comment that he is a master at Jedi mind tricks. That, my friends, is Ego gone awry—plain and simple. All the money in the world cannot fix that. His Ego has him convinced that everyone is against him if they are not fervently on his side—his art of the deal. This has taken years to develop to this degree, and sadly, it is doubtful that anyone could ever help him at this point in his life.

My point in all this is—do not let your Egos remove all common decency and respect for one another, for it is not a recipe for success. The 2016 GOP nominee appears successful despite himself, and I would only use his actions as an example of what not to do if you wish to live a life of peace and harmony. I wish not to judge him, only to point out how harmful the Ego can become if left unchecked.

CHAPTER 4

What if human evolution had help?

The Ant Farm: Who Are the Aliens?

Except for my out-of-body experience, my mother has always had a very open mind when it comes to the questions of our existence and our abilities. Early on, she would half joke that it was highly likely that we were nothing more than ants in an ant farm, put here by some higher being—or maybe even aliens that we couldn't see because they were out of our realm of perception. I would say, "Nah-ah! No way!" And she would tease, saying, "How do you know?" So I began thinking about the ants in the ant farm. They were so small in comparison to our world that they virtually had no idea or concept of us human beings, much less our world—the perspective would be too vast for them to consider. The same could be said of our understanding of Heaven if we were to think of Heaven as a place. It would be so far outside the realm of our understanding that we would not be able to observe it, even if it were located on our physical plain of existence and ready for us to observe. Think about how difficult it is for us to perceive our own Milky Way galaxy, much less our Universe. In fact, until telescopes were invented, we were not even aware of much of our own solar system.

A phenomenon best illustrates the ant farm. I am not sure if the phenomenon actually has a name, so let's just call it *invisible ships*. It refers to the arrival of Christopher Columbus's ships to the new world and how, supposedly, the natives were unable to see his ships docked in their harbor. The theory is that the Indians did not have the mental capacity or experience to process such a sight, and therefore the ships were made invisible to them, or at least did not pose a threat. The context was so foreign that they saw nothing to relate to. Even if some of them had actually seen something, they had no point of reference from which to identify the ships, so the ships were, in fact, not relevant. The ships had no meaning and therefore had no value for their minds. The same could be said of the ants in the ant farm. Everything outside their little world is too much to experience for it to make sense for them as it is completely out of their perspective. So, one could argue that—for many humans—the Universe is quite the same experience in the physical realm. Moreover, it is impossible for us to reckon with Heaven because Heaven is completely devoid of form to contrast with, and we humans must have contrast in order to make sense of things.

For many people, modern technology only makes matters worse because it proves just how vast the Universe really is—as if it didn't seem big enough before. Think about how long it took for mankind to understand that we are part of something larger than a solar system, a galaxy, and that our tiny planet called Earth orbits around just one of a billion stars in our galaxy. For thousands of years, we were barely aware that we were part of a solar system. Moreover, what do the billion other stars look like in our galaxy? They look like nothing, just like Columbus's ship in the harbor. But now, we have the lenses (technology) to see so far enough into our known Universe that we can actually count (with the aid of advanced computers) billions of galaxies within our Universe, and we already estimate there are billions of stars in each galaxy. For those of you science geeks reading this, it is estimated that there are 10^{24} planet-like objects (1,000,000,000,000,000,000,000,000) in our observable Universe. At this point, we stop trying to comprehend our significance, like the little ants in the ant farm or the natives on the shoreline. We have no perspective beyond anything that's not directly in front of us. Mother's analogy about the ant farm and God is, of course, obvious. She could have easily suggested that God put us here as some kind of display or perhaps some kind of an experiment. And she could be right about the aliens. I mean, for all we know, we could very well be an experiment of some far-off alien species.

Many people believe that our DNA has been engineered by a higher intelligence of some kind—and not since antiquity, but very recently in our evolution. One might equate this to the missing link. The unique ability of human beings to speak was recently found to be related to a rare and advanced FOXP2 gene, and many question why this gene only developed in Homo sapiens. Its origins have, thus far, not been found—so how did we obtain it? Moreover, scientists are fairly certain that only 3 percent of the DNA contained in our genetic makeup is responsible for reproduction, and the remainder is currently undecipherable. I contend that the remaining 97 percent is a vast library, perhaps housing the answers to all life in the Universe, since time and space were created. I also speculate that there might be a component in the DNA of all living beings that enables our spiritual selves to occupy so that upon birth we are already well entrenched in the host that we have chosen.

I envision that DNA is analogous to the grooves on a phonographic record. Until the technology is created or discovered to unravel such imprints, they may remain locked up in a code that is indecipherable. Here's another way of thinking about this. Imagine you are an explorer in the late 16th century, in an era that is marked by profound technical advancements. You set off on an expedition that seeks to find new shipping routes for your country's spice trade. You eventually land on an uncharted island in the middle of the Pacific Ocean in hopes of replenishing dwindling fresh water stores and fresh food. As you explore the island you find a cave. While exploring the caverns within the cave you discover a metal box and inside the box are several discs, made of a light weight material you have never seen before. You are fascinated with their perfectly round shape and thin construction. Each disc has a small hole in the middle with a purpose as yet unknown. Both sides of the disc have some kind of foreign material pasted around the middle with some kind of language imprinted on them, origins unknown. Each side appears different. You find it very odd but understand it must have significance because they are intricate and appear to have a unique purpose and you believe they hold a record of something important. However, you did not find a device nearby that could translate (play) each disc, so you are forced to wait until you return to civilization in order to research what all the strange variations of miniscule notches are that you see engraved on the discs.

Once in a laboratory and upon closer examination with a newly invented microscopic device, you see the circular lines are actually one contiguous groove and inside the groove are various degrees of indentations. The discovery of this indicates a linear message of some kind. It will take you considerable time to relate their purpose and to devise equipment that can read or "play" the phonograph message. Once this is accomplished, you will find that it is some kind of message in a spoken language that has never been heard before. So it will take many more years to construct the message while deciphering the code (language). This analogy could be related to the discovery of our genome and DNA. While we have found the many various strands and sequences, we are still attempting to translate and decipher what much of it means in order to find relevance in it. Thus far, we have only translated a fraction of the information found in human DNA as it relates to our reproduction. It may take many more years of process of elimination, or new technology, in order to achieve this.

Giorgio A. Tsoukalos, television personality and contributor on the History Channel's Ancient Aliens program, is quoted as saying on the show; *"DNA is the most powerful storage device in the Universe. Not even with all the modern supercomputers combined in the world could we store as much information as we could store on DNA."*[14] If this is indeed true, we humans are certainly more than meets the eye.

What about Faith?

Faith, when referring to God, is best defined as one's belief in something based on spiritual comprehension rather than physical proof. It is intangible. Faith is the act of believing in something without tangible evidence of it. The best example I can give is when we ask ourselves if our parents love us. When we answer, "Yes, of course my parents love(d) me," (and hopefully they do/did) if asked to prove it, we might find it difficult, citing numerous examples of their behavior to support why we think our parents love us. However, we cannot provide tangible proof that our parents love us. It is a personal, intangible, and visceral feeling. We rely on faith that it is so, so that we feel their love.

It is the same with believing there is a God, that He created us, and that we are His children. You do not know this for sure, but you might have a good feeling this is so. Similar to your parent's love, God is just as intangible. Most religions would have you believe in Him (or some other deity) relying on just your faith alone. So where does that faith really come from? It likely comes from centuries of reading our ancient texts, which instill in us that faith alone is our salvation.

Personally, my faith only goes so far. Sure, I have faith there is a God, but I have issues with the original authors' and scribes' understanding of God as written in many of our ancient texts. I also take issue with how they translated ancient texts such as the Holy Bible and the Quran, for example. I will expound upon this more in chapter 9 when I discuss religion and politics, but suffice it to say, my belief is one based upon logic, not based on what our ancient ancestors interpreted thousands of years ago.

While I have humored biblical notions of faith in God as they have been written, I have ultimately come to the conclusion that God did not create our Universe—we did. And I don't mean *we* as in human entities, I mean *we spiritual entities*. This notion requires another—more profound—explanation, however. This is where logic must kick in. I think we can all agree with science that the Universe and our world were not created in seven days, so I think that my reluctance to interpret everything the Bible says literally is founded upon a logical apprehension. Another example is that, according to biblical tradition, some will say, the world began in 4,000BC, and yet we now know that to be at least many thousands of years later than the actual dating of the ruins of Göbekli Tepe, the archaeological site discovered in Turkey in 1963. This even predates Ur, the Mesopotamian ancient civilization thought to be the birthplace of humanity. Therefore, it's hard for the Bible to maintain integrity when its facts can be contradicted by such historical and technological discovery and especially with carbon dating verification.

Science will maintain that all the right ingredients to create life were present in our carbon-rich Universe at the time of the so-called big bang. Isn't that interesting? All the right ingredients were present at the very beginning—but were they, really? What we know scientifically is that it took billions of years for carbon to form in our Universe because it would take a massive star to create carbon, and it was calculated to have taken billions of years for the early expansion of the Universe to create such massive stars capable of collapsing and forming carbon. Now, think about this for a minute. If God is the almighty being that we think of, why would it take billions of years for Him just to create carbon? In fact, why would it take a full seven days to create the Heavens and the Earth? If God had anything to do with our Universe, wouldn't He have made it so in an instant? Or does time in the Universe work differently, depending upon your size and place in it—the way time works for ants in the ant farm? It is perhaps easier to understand this by studying time as presented in the "Cosmic Calendar" by Carl Sagan in his extraordinary book *The Dragons of Eden*[15].

So, my question is—what did our spiritual brothers and sisters (or co-Creators) do to kill time until they would have the right stuff in order to ultimately create us? I hazard a guess that their first intentions were not to create human beings at all. My theory is that our initial desires were only to experience contrast, but out of those desires, we inadvertently created a physical world of form in order to facilitate the business of comparing that contrast. Then we needed a life-form with the physical senses to be able to observe the contrast.

So, our new Egos had convinced us that we had created the first mortal sin. We had left the proverbial Garden of Eden. We were runaways. We had separated from God. Therefore, the expanding Universe was a convenient place to hide out so that God could not come after us with his wrath and scorn for what we had done. "A-ha! You see?" you may say. "Maybe this is why so many religions present God as a vengeful and judgmental God!"

Under this hypothesis, I can see why most of us think that God is a vengeful and judgmental God. As such, we have been programmed to believe that we are sinners and that we must be punished! However, this is not true. God does not subscribe to this dream that we call our physical reality. Our world is illusionary, and as such, God has no interest in it except for His concern for our return home. God's primary interest is in our souls, not our illusionary dreams.

Remember: our Egos have to be the heroes, protecting us from the wrath and scorn of God. Ego has also made sure we believe and have faith in this—to the point where we have written it into our holy books. We believe that, because we feel that we have separated from God and we have allowed Ego's help to hide and protect us. Similarly, we hide behind many words in our ancient texts because they have become familiar and make us feel safe. We have enabled our Ego to help create a world in which to hide. Ego is a sounding board—something we secretly deliberate with, confide in, and expect counsel from. This has become a dangerous investment for humankind. We depend far too much on Ego's counsel, advice which far exceeds our need to survive in this world that we had created. Dream or not, we have many actors in this play, and some may not be acting in our best interests.

Another important understanding about the ant farm analogy is that it was easy for us to hide by becoming microscopic in the scheme of things. We are like the ants in the ant farm. They are so small that their Universe is only the farm itself—the actual sand caves they live in. They know nothing of the world outside of their anthill. So (if they can even sense fear) they must feel safe and protected. We have done the same thing in our realities, and this is one reason most of us do not wish to explore beyond our world. Staying small and ignorant makes us feel safe! It is the same with what we believe when we read the Bible. Keeping to the holy script makes us feel safe. It's what we know!

What about the Ancient-Aliens Theory?

There are plenty of ancient-aliens theorists who contend that our current state of affairs—the evolution of human intelligence and the technology that we possess—must have been transplanted here on Earth. I already alluded to this, but here is another reason why.

Many scientists believe it is theoretically impossible for us to have evolved to the point at which we find ourselves today. One such scientist is astronomer Fred Hoyle, who perhaps invented the "Junkyard tornado" analogy in his analysis of evolution. According to Hoyle's analysis, the probability of cellular life evolving was extremely low and he commented;

> *"The chance that higher life forms might have emerged in this way is comparable to the chance that a tornado sweeping through a junkyard might assemble a Boeing 747 from the materials therein."*

Hoyle goes on to reflect;

> *"Life as we know it is, among other things, dependent on at least 2000 different enzymes. How could the blind forces of*

the primal sea manage to put together the correct chemical elements to build enzymes?"

Hoyle used this to argue in favor of panspermia, that the origin of life on Earth had come from preexisting life in space."

We live in a technological age. We communicate with one another via computers, whether that be a PC, tablet, or smartphone. No longer do we depend upon carrier pigeons or the Pony Express for long-distance communications. We've traded the anxiety of less-than-dependable forms of communication for today's fast-paced lifestyle and the angst of responding to a multitude of correspondence requiring immediate attention. Ideas and information are being shared at breathtaking speeds today, enabling human beings to collaborate much more efficiently, and hence, intelligently. I suspect our brain power has also increased as a direct result of our more efficient forms of communication.

As shared by Giorgio Tsoukalos on one of the History Channel's Ancient Aliens shows, "One minute we were sitting in caves, and the next minute we were building pyramids. This quantum leap can only be explained with a direct extraterrestrial intervention in our past." While critics may see his line of thinking as a bit over the top, Mr. Tsoukalos makes his arguments by asking "and who could deny the improbability that mankind would go from horse and buggy to the moon in less than one hundred years?" What if Moore's Law[16] applies, which states that processor speeds, or overall processing power for computers will double every two years. What if this theory should be extended to evolution and human intelligence in general?

Those who contend that this accident could not have happened without intervention are not alone. Many ancient-alien theorists believe that the advanced intelligence of such notable icons as Leonardo de Vinci, Albert Einstein, J. Robert Oppenheimer, Wernher von Braun, and Nikola Tesla had to have been influenced by other worldly beings with a much higher intelligence. So why has there been no scientific investigation to explain such genius? Why is there only speculation about such advancements? Are our Egos so large that we do not wish to reveal that we have had help from other worldly beings? Or are our Egos so large we think we did it all on our own? Here's a thought; what if the so-called "other worldly beings" of influence are simply our own spiritual brothers and sisters trying to help us progress? And, what if they are actually doing it through upgrades to our DNA, where we humans can tap into this stream of knowledge subconsciously?

Some would say such wild advancements in our technology are not widely spoken of because there is not enough scientific evidence to explain it. I contend there is the public fear factor, just as in ancient times when Jesus was freaking everyone out with his supernatural abilities. As for extraterrestrial visitations, there is evidence today that governments around the world have covered up such visitations on Earth and refuse to announce or share this activity for fear of public panic. Not surprisingly, there have been plenty of Hollywood movies to illustrate the notion that we are not alone in the cosmos. But why would extraterrestrials wish to jump-start our technological advances? What if we are being used in some kind of experiment? But without being presented with more factual data, this is what we are left with—pure speculation.

Evidence of extraterrestrial influence can be found all over the planet. Take the prehistoric stone monoliths called Stonehenge, erected more than 4,000 years ago, consisting of more than one hundred stone blocks— some weighing over five tons. Blue stones were brought in from over one hundred miles away from the Prescelly Mountains in Wales. To this day, it is unclear how any humans of that time could have carried stones of that size through the mountains and valleys, across all the rivers and rough terrain to get to England from Wales. We cannot know how Stonehenge was built because human beings were not recording history yet. Some claim in Arthurian legends that Merlin, King Arthur's magician, moved the stones by levitation. And levitation seems to be a good explanation for how the Egyptian pyramids were also built—but there is also no evidence for exactly how *that* was done. Yet Stonehenge is dwarfed by a much larger megalithic site called Avebury. Only seventeen miles away from Stonehenge, Avebury contains the largest stone circle site in the world, with stones weighing between twenty and fifty tons each. Regardless of why they were built, I think it is obvious that, once again, human beings had help from extraterrestrial beings who possessed superior technology.

Just look closely at some of these astounding archeological sites around the world—the great Egyptian pyramids, Pumapunku in Bolivia, the ruins of Machu Picchu in Peru, and El Castillo in Chichen Itza, Mexico. At Pumapunku, we find huge stones that appear to have been laser-cut and laser-drilled into interlocking blocks of equal dimensions—truly higher technology than we have today. Some believe the architects, whomever they were, also melted the stones in place at many of these sites—again, using an unknown technology we currently do not possess.

Erich von Däniken, one of the most profound cosmo-archeologic[4] writers of our time, first introduced the idea that extraterrestrial beings have been visiting and influencing humankind for thousands of years. His thoughtful approach, as reflected in his first novel *Chariots of the Gods*, presents his subject matter in the form of a question—a genius way of saying, *I'm not 100 percent sure of this, so what do you think?* What von Däniken does in his novels is point out these astonishing, seemingly nonhuman accomplishments, and ask his audience to try and explain how their construction might have been possible. Von Däniken—like my uncle—is not satisfied with leaving such questions unanswered, taking investigations about these phenomenal sites one step further by supplying possible extraterrestrial influences to explain them.

The core takeaway that I got from *Chariots of the Gods* is basically summed up in the title. If we were living in a time where our current technology was as primitive as it was, say, 4,000 years ago, we probably would assume the same when seeing machines enter our atmosphere and fly around in our skies. We might indeed see them as the chariots for visiting Gods. Early depictions in cave drawings and stone carvings of such visitations show fire and smoke from objects we would consider engines of some kind. But since these were created thousands of years before the development of a combustion engine of any kind, we would have to come up with some explanation in our renderings such as chariots or magic carpets.

Moreover, I have noticed that a vast majority of ancient renderings of "the Gods", from many different cultures and civilizations, were shown with wings or transported on wings. Again, this makes perfect sense from the standpoint of reference, because, from a point of reference, the only

---

4   My made-up word to fit my description of people like Erich von Däniken, who has tied ancient aliens with archeology.

thing that ancient observers could equate with things flying through the air would be birds! Therefore, we see many ancient cave drawings and hieroglyphs, as well as stone carvings and statues, showing such deities as having wings. Perhaps our primeval "angels" were seen flying, so they naturally got portrayed with wings as well.

Now, most people today understand that whatever special, or extra-terrestrial, beings were witnessed and memorialized thousands of years ago did not actually have wings. But flew they did in some form of craft and wings were the only explanation of how this was possible. And of course, they must be Gods or demons for there was no concept for aliens.

I appreciate how von Däniken appropriately questions—*if they were Gods, then why would they need a contraption to fly around in to begin with? If they were Gods, why would they visit us in a vehicle that would likely scare the crap out of us?* I wholeheartedly agree with von Däniken in his assessment that his God (my God as well) does not need a ship to fly around in. Moreover, if God came to Earth to visit He would not do so in such an upsetting, and mostly frightening, manner. This should be all the evidence we need that they were not Gods; so what were they? Still, this mistaken identity does not take away from the interpretation our ancestors had thousands of years ago. In all likelihood, they must have been scared out of their wits and willing to submit to any form of servitude in order to appease such 'Gods.' I suspect that if the Egyptian pyramids were built using slaves, there would have been good reason to submit to their wishes because it is reasonable to assume that with that form of advanced technology also came weapons of mass destruction.

Given all the evidence of ancient aliens using and planting superior technology on the planet, it would be easy to speculate that aliens have been also tampering with our DNA in order to expedite our human progress. Ancient-alien theorists are split on the reasons why. Some believe it has been to help the human race, while others believe our DNA has been tinkered with for selfish purposes. Of course, this opens up a Pandora's box as to purpose and motive.

Suffice it to say, it looks as if we have had help. This will give some critics of Charles Darwin's theory of evolution[17] much to revel in. And while I do believe in Darwin's theory, I do believe there were periods in our evolution that were advanced by supernatural intervention. As astronomer

Philip Imborgno has said, *"There's no explanation for human beings. They shouldn't be here on this planet."* Moreover, a study in 2004 by researchers at the Howard Hughes Medical Institute at the University of Chicago indicated that the sophistication of the human brain was the result of a special event. They postulate that the genes of humans went through an intense amount of change in a relatively short amount of time. This is referred to as the big bang of the Brain[18]. What if extraterrestrials have been here to speed up our evolutionary progress? If that is true, it would most likely have required some type of time travel. Because, why would more advanced beings have come here in the distant past to advance our cause if they could not come back thousands of years later (or go back in time) to check in on us? Why give our species on planet Earth the boost we needed to get to the evolutionary place we find ourselves in today? Certainly, there must be an ulterior motive.

And Time travel? While quantum mechanics may explain how this is theoretically possible with a concept of bending time and space, most of us humans lack the intelligence to understand it. And that's not to say that we are stupid. The fact is, most intelligent beings filter their stored knowledge, generally limiting this storage to only what is required for survival. It does not mean we are stupid. Our survival would not require an understanding of quantum mechanics or string theory. For most of us, all we need is a GPS to get us from here to there, and we do not need to know how it works! Understand that our immediate ancestors relied on compasses and crude maps to get from point A to point B, but they were happy to have that. It is all a matter of perspective. Our children's children will probably laugh that we had to depend upon a GPS. However, we may ultimately end up developing the technology for time travel if we continue our aspirations for exploring space, for this cannot be done with our current chemical propulsion technology, which can only move us at a rate of up to 24,000 mph. Time travel would have to surpass or exceed the speed of light (186,000 mi/sec or 669,600,000 mph). While I understand that it may be possible for humans to travel at or close to the speed of light, even if we can overcome the traumas to the human body created by inertia, I do not believe this will even get us close to the concept of time travel. So another technology must be found outside our current form of known propulsion.

The Sitchin Theory

Here is another take. What if we humans are not the direct results of our creation in this Universe, but by-products of it? Let us suppose for a minute that the super-intelligent aliens are the ones who imagined this time-space reality, and that we are their little experiments. In fact, there are some who describe how our original Earthly hominids were used in genetic experimentation, and how humans are the result of successful gene splicing, possibly by the Anunnaki. Zecharia Sitchi[19] speculates—through collective archeological evidence and ancient mythology—that ancient Sumerian-Babylonian Gods, the Anunnaki, are aliens from the planet Nibiru (Sitchin's Twelfth Planet). Sitchin says that this planet passes by the Earth every 3,500 years or so, at which time they planet-hop to the Earth and create mischief[20]. Sounds like a Star Trek plot. But seriously, Sitchin wrote that they first arrived on Earth probably 450,000 years ago, looking for minerals—especially gold—which they found and mined in Africa. Sitchin states that these "Gods" were the rank-and-file workers of the colonial expedition to Earth from planet Nibiru. He also suggested that to relieve the Anunnaki, who had mutinied over their dissatisfaction with their working conditions, primitive workers (Homo sapiens) were genetically engineered to create slaves to replace the Anunnaki in the gold mines. These slaves were created by crossing extraterrestrial genes with those of Homo erectus.

According to Sitchin, ancient inscriptions report that the human civilization in Sumer, Mesopotamia was organized under the guidance of these "Gods." Human kingship was inaugurated to provide intermediaries between mankind and the Anunnaki (creating the Divine Right of Kings doctrine). I would add that this may have been the first use of a hierarchical order, albeit human, so that the masses would follow one of their own; a king, a ruler, or a director of sorts.

Sitchin believes that fallout from nuclear weapons used during a war between factions of the extraterrestrials is the "evil wind"—described in the *Lament for Ur*—that destroyed Ur around 2000 BC. Sitchin states the exact year is 2024 BC. Sitchin says that his research coincides with many biblical texts and that biblical texts come originally from Sumerian writings. Ur was an important Sumerian city-state in ancient Mesopotamia, located at the site of modern Tell el-Muqayyar in south Iraq's Dhi Qar

Governorate[21]. Many important ancient artifacts from Mesopotamia have been discovered in Ur, which is considered the "cradle of civilization."

Of course, this is all somewhat speculative, but piecing together our ancient history has always been a challenge. What I am certain of is this—we are who we are today because we are eternal. This has been given many names—eternal spirits, souls, energy, vibration, life-force, Source Energy—many labels for many masters. So how did we evolve to this point in time?

Again, I believe it was through our DNA! We are a part of physical life through our DNA. We use DNA to accumulate knowledge and pass it along from generation to generation in all life-forms. What if the Anunnaki understood this and were responsible for accelerating our intelligence and other capabilities through our DNA? We are able to achieve a little bit more from incarnation to incarnation through our stored experiences. Over time, this can translate into instinct, which I believe is also stored in our DNA and helps life-forms adapt and mutate to survive in the environment in which they find themselves.

Certainly, this is how evolution works in plants and animals on our planet—through the addition of information in our DNA. DNA information is what makes us who we are, physically. Since this is the part of our DNA that we have not been able to dissect, the question remains— how was some of this information introduced into human DNA to make us technologically superior to all other animals on the planet? For this reason, and because of this unanswered question, I no longer believe that outer space will be our final frontier. I believe that we may find even more answers to our origins from the exploration of our inner space. Genetics and DNA would be the best places to start.

This gets us back to the ant farm—so perhaps mom was right all along! Most living things, regardless of species, are normally only concerned with their current circumstances and immediate surroundings, just like the ants. Therefore, it really is a matter of perspective, and, once again, our founding doctrine of contrasting. The ant is only concerned with his ant farm. The anteater is only concerned with the ant farms in his domain. The mountain lion is only concerned with his territory full of anteaters. And so on—ever expanding territories of concern and observation, depending upon the level of perspective and contrast they live in. Eventually human beings may be—and well should be—concerned with the domain of the entire planet, since we are the highest level of intelligence on the planet and have the ability to affect everything on it.

As of this writing—and sadly to admit—we humans have yet to take responsibility for the well-being of planet Earth. We seem to believe that it runs on a perpetual clock, never requiring winding or care of any kind. Let us hope it is not too late and that the collective human experience on planet Earth will realize its role in protecting our planet before it is too late!

The Catch-22

I believe that we (spirits) created the physical world, and *we* created a physical human being in which to experience this world, in all its form. The irony is that we created all this physical stuff just so that we could experience the contrast of it. It is kind of like testing how unbreakable a new metal alloy is by trying to break it. At some point it will break—then what? On to something more unbreakable?

So we got the contrast we wished for—now what? Has this brought about a revelation as to our relationship with God? Perhaps not, but why is that? Because we created a false tool (physical reality) with which to measure that which is not measurable. What if we only created a world of contrast in which to set out and play in? Remember: we were simply innocent minds with the keen ability to create. So what to do with this amazing capability?

Unfortunately, it seems that we have not thought ahead to the consequences of creating an alternate Universe of physicality. The fact that the physical Universe in which we live in is ever expanding might be proof that this world has no end—until, perhaps, we all get tired of playing in it. Physical matter is a paradox. No matter how hard we try, we may never find the endgame. The microscopic world will simply appear smaller and smaller, and the macroscopic world will appear larger and larger. We will simply keep inventing new tools with which to explore further inward and outward, but we will be forever stuck trying to find the endgame because that is the nature of contrast. What if this is also the nature of God? Perhaps our lesson is that there is no beginning, and there is no end to any of it. We never really die.

CHAPTER 5

What if universal laws govern attraction?

In fact, what if such attractive forces created the Universe itself, primal forces called *intentions*?

The Power of Attraction and the Power of Intention.

Think for a moment of things we humans create on a daily basis. Does anyone believe that our creations do not stem from original intents to create? And, is it not true that, oftentimes, our intentions are born from our dream of *what if*? One thing that I have noticed during my life is that most successful people are not afraid to dream and dream big.

Law of attraction is key to the New Thought philosophy, and it is an underlying component in the success of prosperous people all over the world. It is the belief that like energy attracts like energy—and thus, the power of attraction can work both ways. Take for example people who seem down on their luck or are unhappy. You will find that they unwittingly attract that experience into their lives because it is what they focus upon the most.

Successful people have harnessed the power of attraction by focusing on what they want, not what they do not want. They also develop a mantra of gratitude for the things they already have, no matter how small and insignificant. Gratitude is an essential component in the law of attraction.

Law of attraction principles are universal and are so profound that Esther and Jerry Hicks wrote a book in 1981 on the subject called *Law of Attraction*[22] This spawned a series of other inspirational books surrounding the universal laws of attraction. Laws on the power of attraction are behind the book *The Secret* by Rhonda Byrne[23]. It is no coincidence that Esther and Jerry Hicks (and Abraham) also appear in Rhonda's original movie under the same title. According to Esther and Jerry Hicks, "Abraham"[24], consists of a group of entities which are "interpreted" by Esther Hicks. Abraham described themselves as "a group consciousness from the non-physical dimension". Abraham-Hicks is a dynamic relationship of teacher and translator. Along similar lines, *The Power of Intention* by Dr. Wayne Dyer[25] illuminates these universal laws of attraction by focusing on our intent to accomplish things. It seems natural that the more energy we put behind our intentions, the more likely we will have success in accomplishing those intentions.

My observation is that successful people are not afraid to fail. Arguably, one of the most successful people at failing in America is, by his own account, Thomas Edison. In a conversation between Thomas Edison and Walter Mallory surrounding the failures of Edison's nickel-iron battery tests, Mallory commented [to Edison], *"Isn't it a shame that with the tremendous amount of work you have done, you haven't been able to get any results?"* Mallory reports, "Edison turned on me like a flash, and with a smile replied, *Results! Why, man, I have gotten a lot of results! I know several thousand things that won't work."*[26]

My observation is that successful people likely grew up with a support group of family, friends, teachers, and clergy who all said, "You can do anything you set your mind to. Go for it!" Encouragement programming, otherwise known as positive reinforcement, is a great kick-starter for success but not a guarantee. Likewise, those of us who have not accomplished what we have wished in life may have grown up with a lack of support and encouragement and probably heard, "Get your head out of the clouds, and be realistic. You will never get that done!" It goes both ways, and yet there are exceptions that defy the odds. There are those of us who will take that negativity and turn it around. Such people are fighters against all odds and refuse to take no for an answer. They seem to have an internal coach, perhaps Ego, egging them on, keeping them going. The power of attraction is an amazing gift that we human Creators possess, which as I have said previously, our Creator originally bestowed upon us. When we tap into Source Energy, we possess the power to move mountains. According to Abraham-Hicks,

Source Energy is intimately, infinitely, always responding to your requests, no matter how great or small they may be deemed by you or anyone else who is observing them. There is nothing so big that Source Energy can't get its thoughts around it—and there is nothing so small that Source Energy isn't willing to get its thoughts around it. [27]

The successful people of this world understand that. They've obviously found that spigot of potential. Moreover, they've found the way to open it and use it, over and over again. And people will always ask—what is their secret?

Time and time again, Abraham-Hicks reminds us human,

"You are extensions of Non-physical Energy, taking thought beyond which it has been before, and through contrast, you will come to conclusions or decision. And once you align with your desire, the Energy that creates worlds will flow through you … which means enthusiasm and passion and triumph. **That is your destiny.***"* [28]

I would take that one step further and center that a bit on absolute faith. Do you have faith or confidence that you can create worlds, accomplish your goals? Having faith in your intention allows you to see it so without proof that it can be so. Like many good architects, you see the finished project even before putting the outline to paper. This vision originates from the nonphysical energy that we are connected to and can all tap into at any time. Your success-rate is equal to your faith-rate. When your faith-rate is lowered by doubts, your success rate will mirror that. So even if you finish a project that you set out to complete, you may stumble and falter in the process when your faith-rate is not 100 percent. So the next time you begin a new project, accept that any kinks and snags that may pop up in the process are just steps toward completion. Do not be discouraged by such obstacles and instead view them positively as building blocks. Fighting such obstacles may feed more of the negative energy which brought them into the fold in the first place. Instead, use your energy to address these as just part of the plan!

Barry Holstun Lopez, American author, is quoted as saying, *"It is the imagination that gives shape to the Universe."*[29] I think Mr. Lopez's quote sums up my own philosophy very nicely, since I believe *we* created the Universe from our strong desire for contrast. That desire was translated into imagination, which is an undeniable quality that we all possess. The Universe did not exist until we imagined it. This should be an exciting concept for us as there is basically nothing that we cannot accomplish (sorry for the double negative).

Understand that it all comes down to focus and intent. So ask yourself -- what is my focus in a given situation? Haphazard attention on any project increases the likelihood for some kind of failure. You cannot expect a perfect outcome for your goals if your attention is willy-nilly, no matter how strong your initial intent was. To be successful in a given project you must:

1. See the results or finished project clearly.
2. Map out the project from start to finish.
3. Identify and assign the appropriate resources.
4. Anticipate potential roadblocks and plan for alternatives.

I wish to make it clear that, while step D is important, planning alternatives should never be a primary focus unless you actually need to carry out the alternatives instead of the primary objective. This can be a normal part of the process, as some decisions cannot be made ahead of time, and unknown variables may be part of the mix. Always remember— be mindful what you wish for. Thinking about a subject for any length of time is equivalent to wishing for it. What you think about the most becomes your predominant thought, and the Universe will generally deliver upon that. So, if your intent is plan A, then do not spend much time thinking about plan B unless you are willing to sacrifice your original intent and end up with plan B. It truly is your choice, but you must be clear on what you want while eliminating all of the things that you do not want from your thought process.

So whether your desire is to build an addition to your house or to increase the amount of money that you have in the bank, your focus on that desire must be undeniable. Again, if you focus on possible obstacles by thinking of all the things that may keep you from obtaining more money, for example, then you will certainly not see more money. This is because the Universe of energy that you will be attracting will be haphazard at best. Do not muddy the waters with too many choices. Your intent cannot be clear as mud. Clarity of purpose is essential. Therefore, find your highest purpose and stick to it.

The power of intention is a very powerful thing. Set by desire, an alignment with Source Energy can be an unyielding source of potential for us to tap into. A big part of our potential is knowing that a thing can be accomplished long before it is manifested, because only then can the appropriate energy be put into the manifestation of it with clear intent. Consider a freight train running at sixty miles per hour—its potential (inertia) is seemingly boundless and very hard to stop. So is our potential to create and manifest. Abundance is a natural by-product of this ability to manifest and create.

Abundance and Lack

The feeling of lack and limitation, on the other hand, act as brakes, stopping our natural progressions to create. Doubt is a silent killer of our goals. Little accomplishment can come from the greatest idea when there are thoughts present that it may not be possible, or that you are not worthy to attain it. Source energy is a magnet for desire when it is focused upon with clear intent and not confusing contrary ideas or thoughts. At best, Source Energy, will be confused as to which idea to align with, and your success with it will very much depend upon how much thought and energy you have focused on either its success or its failure. An idea so important cannot have opposition to success—it must be born from positive intention. This is the power of intention.

The most successful people in the world spend very little time considering failure or their worthiness to succeed. On the contrary, the energy spent by successful people is on visualizing their success beforehand and taking the steps necessary to manifest and accomplish those desires. It is always positive energy. To them, failure is not an option, and therefore, it is not a thought within their manifestation energy stream.

Successful people have little doubt or negative energy to spend on their creations. They look at obstacles as just another part of the project plan and welcome the opportunity to bend, adapt, and go with the flow. Another important observation I have regarding successful people is the joy they find throughout the process. They try to find enjoyment in all aspects of their manifestations. The joy they feel translates into gratitude, and the Universe will simply align with that stream of energy and deliver more of that.

Lack and limitation are qualities that are easy to avoid, but you must make an effort. You must eliminate all doubt and fear from your mind. Develop a mantra that *I am worthy*, and *I have all that I need in order to be successful*. Again, you must eliminate all limiting thoughts from your mind. No more thinking negative thoughts like, *I'm not strong enough*, or *I'm not smart enough*, or, *I'm not rich enough*, or *I'm not tall enough*. Standing at only four feet five inches tall, do you think Peter Dinklage thinks he's not tall enough? His success as an actor surely indicates that he believes that he has what it takes to succeed, or he would not be where he is today—one of the most successful adult actors on *Game of Thrones*. So it is obvious that his height, or lack thereof, is not a negative factor in his belief system, and I believe he sees himself just as tall as anyone else does. One thing is for certain, Peter Dinklage does not focus on that which may be perceived as a negative, and thus his height has not become a setback to him. So, how do you see yourself?

You can turn a limitation into an asset if you will simply change your mind about it. Take a limiting thought, and turn it around to your advantage. Do whatever it takes to either eliminate the limiting thought or change your mind about its limit in the first place. Anything negative in your thinking will only serve to bring more of that into your experience. No one likes a pity party and not many people like being dragged into the drama of someone else's troubles. So if you do not have many friends, take a hard look at how you approach people. What predominant thoughts do you share with them? Do you end up speaking about what is wrong with you or what is wrong with life or the world? If so, examine your conversations with people and ask yourself—if I were on the other side of that conversation, would I want to hear more of that in the future? Chances are, if you are honest in your assessment, the answer would be no, because you will likely find that your conversations generally take on a woe-is-me tone.

Generally, if you speak positively and find positive, uplifting topics to converse about, other people will look forward to spending time with you in the future. If your conversations are boring or depressing, they will avoid you in the future. If you find that this is the case, make an effort to stop talking about what is wrong with life and find things that are good and share those instead. Most importantly, try to surround yourself with positive, uplifting people. Make conscious efforts to observe the behavior of others and avoid those who seem more attracted to speaking about negative people, issues, and ideas. Avoid negative people like the plague!

Gratitude: Our True Power for Prosperity

What if prosperity is a birthright?

When we finally understand abundance and accept our inherent right to prosperity, we should see the good in everything, and gratitude should prevail. In that graciousness, the affirmation of all that is good will coalesce and multiply out of the energy in which it was created. Gratitude is a key component in our power to attract prosperity.

Being gracious is like paying that positive energy forward. When you show appreciation for those things that bring you joy, those in receipt of your gratitude can hardly go forward without wanting to exemplify your graciousness. It's like giving a new pair of shoes to someone you care about. They don't even have to fit that person. That person can, in turn, re-gift those shoes to someone else who they care about who may fit them. Ultimately, the gift and the love with which they were given can never be lost. It's like the gift that keeps on giving! So be grateful when you receive a gift that you have no use for because you can always re-gift it to someone who may have use for it.

Gratitude is the purest form of amplification of what is good, what is working in your life. Even the smallest of gifts are positive energy in motion. When you show gratitude for them, you are amplifying and performing a recirculation of the positive energy that was brought to you in the first place. Showing gratitude is our way of refueling the fire, like saying, "Yeah, this feels good, bring it on!" The thought waves created by graciousness are a power-provoking beacon that attracts more of the same. Think of it this way—*like attracts like according to our dominant vibrations.* Gratitude always resonates a positive vibration.

According to Happify Daily,

> *"The benefits of practicing gratitude are nearly endless. People who regularly practice gratitude by taking time to notice and reflect upon the things they're thankful for experience more positive emotions, feel more alive, sleep better, express more compassion and kindness, and even have stronger immune systems. And gratitude doesn't need to be reserved only for momentous occasions. Sure, you might express gratitude after receiving a promotion at work, but you can also be thankful for something as simple as a delicious piece of pie."*[30]

Ask and it is Given!

An important lesson that I have learned is that the Universe is not aware of the gravity or weight of what's behind your gratitude. It is only concerned with amplifying that which brought you the joy for which you are grateful.

Let us say you are struggling financially. You are having a difficult time making ends meet and do not have enough money in the bank to pay all of your bills. Being down and miserable about that troubling reality is not going to turn things around for you. It is not going to bring you prosperity if you keep despairing and focusing on what you do not have, for the Universe will simply pick up on that and bring you more of that poverty and despair.

In Esther and Jerry Hicks' excellent book *Ask and It is Given*, they share, once again, the beautiful teachings of Abraham. I love their description in chapter 16;

> *"If you have the ability to imagine it, or even to think about it, this Universe has the ability and the resources to deliver it fully unto you, for this Universe is like a well-stocked kitchen with every ingredient imaginable at your disposal."*[31]

I think that pretty much sums it up. The Universe of Source Energy has everything you need. If you want to improve any negative or less than optimum situation, you must focus on what you want, not what you do not want. Start with the little things.

So when you find a few dollars in your pants pocket that you didn't know you had, be grateful for the extra cash and do not think, *Well, this isn't going to help me pay the bills!* Instead, be grateful and buy yourself a little lunch, and as you are eating, think grateful thoughts like *I am so prosperous, for this wonderful meal that came out of nowhere!* So what if it's only a hamburger and a drink? The Universe doesn't know the difference. It only knows that it is bringing you joy and the power of attraction will focus on providing more of that.

When it comes to your financial woes, keep thinking positive thoughts like *I know a solution is coming to me soon!* or *I know that more money will present itself in my life very soon!* or *I know I will find opportunities any day now that can enrich my financial situation and benefit my family and myself!* Also, develop mantras like *The right and perfect job is coming my way soon!* and be giddy about it as if it's already in front of you. Such positive affirmations vibrate throughout the ethers. It is related to cause-and-effect energy that has the potential to deliver what you need, but you have to see it already manifested to summon it! Again beware: your mantras must be done with joyous optimism and not done with *oh, what ails me.* Such underlying thoughts of despair will be the overarching factor in what the Universe matches you with.

See it so. See it already done. Be detailed in your vision, but do not limit your vision. Think, *I see this or something better!* It is like an architect who sees his or her house plans in his or her mind long before construction begins. Even before the materials are ordered, the architect's visions are transferred to paper so he or she can fine-tune exactly what he or she wants to build before the first nail is ever driven. After that, construction goes very smoothly, because the exact materials are known (and correctly ordered) ahead of time, and the right human resources can also be adequately planned for its construction. There is no way for the architect to build that perfect house without seeing it first. Oh, sure, he could haphazardly start building without plans. Nevertheless, imagine all the struggles he or she will go through as things don't come together smoothly, not planning for having the right tools when the contractor needs them, and how many times he or she will have to redo something because there are no blueprints to follow.

It is also similar to preparing a good meal to cook. You will have much more success with the meal by developing a list for all the ingredients for the menu ahead of time. Envisioning what it will taste like will enable you to fine-tune the ingredients before a trip to the grocery store. Such envisioning and preparation will add a high probability that the outcome (or what the Universe delivers) is always a match for what you want. And if you cook the meal with love and joy, it is bound to be delicious!

Don't Sweat the Small Stuff!

One day I felt like such a master in my own right. My friend had been whining about some (seemingly) trivial matters in her life and finally it occurred to me to tell her, "Don't sweat the small stuff!" I could not recall where I had heard that, but it was something that has stuck with me throughout my life from early adulthood because of what follows. Don't sweat the small stuff, because you might someday require the energy to deal with something really big and heavy-duty in the future. If you've exhausted a good part of your life sweating the small stuff, you probably won't be capable of handling the really major stuff, like a terminal illness, the decline of a parent, traumatic injury, or the death of a loved one.

The reality is everything is small. We humans have a keen ability to make a mountain out of a molehill. And just like our perceived need for greed (see chapter 7), we need drama in order to validate many aspects in our lives, or, at least, to validate what we are doing in our lives. We humans have gotten pretty good at creating drama to justify just about all our emotions. It is like our Ego needs a story to justify whatever it is that we are doing or feeling, so it creates drama for that. Why am I feeling bad? Because so-and-so did such and such to me. Notice the part about "did to me!" It's never enough that so-and-so did such and such; they had to do it to me! Boom, therein lies the drama. It is no longer about them; it is only about me. Don't look at them; look at me. Feel sorry for me. Take sides with me.

Ego must involve the self, for how else can we engage anyone else in what is happening with ourselves? We cry out for a pity party; we need others to be on our side and feel sorry for us. We need others on our side in support of making us right while simultaneously being the victim. And so look at what really happens. We become the victims of our own subterfuge. We are not really the victim until we begin the drama of convincing others that we are. It is a self-fulfilling prophecy of sorts.

Think of how peaceful our lives would be, however, if we could stop using others as an excuse for what is wrong in our lives. Projecting these pictures of what is wrong is what's wrong in the first place. Moreover, it's exhausting! We should be instead saving our energy for the bigger picture, for the truly heavy burdens that may pop up in our lives. We don't have to be the centers of attention in every moment of our lives. We could instead place compassion for others as an energy-giving quest to give back to society. Be mindful of others with gratitude for what we have and not creating drama for that which is absent. It's not a matter if your glass is half empty or half full, it's how you demonstrate what's in it. I think it is far more appropriate to feel grateful that there is something in my glass to begin with.

I find it rather amusing now to see people being all upset and worked up over some seemingly trifle matter. The sad part is they have no perspective as to how trivial the matter really is. Not finding something to wear in the morning is not something worth getting worked up about. Getting a flat tire on the way to work might be. But getting a flat tire is nothing compared to finding out a close friend or loved one was just killed in a fatal car accident. So even getting a flat tire would be considered sweating the small stuff if you give too much attention to it; it's just a flat tire—get over it!

Try not to create drama about things that do not really matter. Ask yourself: is this situation temporary, or will it require more energy over a longer period of time to deal with it? Not finding the right outfit to wear or getting a flat tire is temporary and not worth your energy to get upset and create drama from. Dealing with the loss of a loved one, or planning to move across country might be better use of your energy in this case. So don't sweat the small stuff!

Loving What Is

Finally, if you are like many who fret over far too many things in life, I highly recommend Byron Katie's book, *Loving What Is*. After reading this insightful book, I was left with a completely different perspective on living day to day. The key takeaway is this. If you are sad, depressed, upset, or angry about something that has already happened, ask yourself what good can come from continuing to focus upon that which has made you sad or upset? It has already happened. Ask yourself, "Can I change something that has already happened?" Of course the answer is always *no*! So, if you cannot change the past, why are you spending any energy on it? Likewise, if you are worried about things yet to happen in the future, ask yourself if worrying about something that has not yet happened is a good use of energy? Even if you falsely answer yes, go back to the universal laws of attraction and understand you will gain nothing by worrying about something before it has happened. The law of attraction may end up bringing that which you are worrying about due to your focus upon it.

The practice of loving what is can be used to avoid struggles, minor turmoil, and arguments, and reminds me of the lesson the willow tree gives us. By bending in the wind instead of standing rigid, the tree is able to go with the flow and avoid snapping under the stress. Loving what is makes life easier, less stressful, and virtually eliminates energy-wasting drama.

Loving what is gives us power and saves us energy. By accepting what is in front of us, and not fighting a given situation, we virtually eliminate the negative drama that always results in a battle. And by not pushing against a perceived problem, you can use your power in the direction of positivity, a much better use of your precious energy. By loving what is, we can live stress-free lives!

Therefore, love what is happening right now; do not sweat the small stuff. Save your energy for positive thoughts and ideas that will benefit you, that can positively transform you. Remember: you cannot change the past, so it makes no sense to dwell upon it. Revisiting something regretful that has already taken place serves you no good purpose and will likely upset you and start a process of drama that can snowball very quickly. Similarly, the future hasn't arrived yet so stop worrying about it. Look forward to the future by holding thoughts of how you would like it to look, not by worrying about how you don't want it to look. By setting positive intentions, your now moments will also be more pleasant, and you will find more joy in the process of making room for what the future may bring. Try to focus most of your thoughts and energy in what's happening right now. This approach has worked well for me in recent years, so I highly recommend it.

Patience

It is worth mentioning, given this time of instant gratification, that it may be counter-intuitive to hold out and wait for the good that you expect and deserve. But good things DO come to those who wait. Like fine wine, you cannot, you must not, rush the good coming to you. The Universe of Source Energy often lays the ground work for the eventual good coming your way, so be patient. In other words, other activities may be necessary as part of this groundwork. This unfolding may not always be immediately obvious to you, but pushing against the stream of energy being presented to you is called resistance, and resistance will usually bring about the opposite effect of your ultimate desire. So be patient and go with the flow being presented. To be sure, continue to offer thoughts of what you want, and you will find that your Source Energy will bring you the comfort and joy you so richly deserve. Just be patient.

So relax. Life is supposed to be fun. Do not allow anxiety to interfere with your energy stream. Anxiety is also resistance, which will always interfere with your well-being. Remember, by loving what is, you can avoid anxiety, so go with the flow, and remember the Willow tree!

CHAPTER 6

What if grief makes us human?

Emotional Pain

Not too long ago, our nation mourned the loss of the son of our (then) vice president. Beau Biden's death was a tragic personal loss for the Biden family. I thought I knew what that meant, but I didn't, not really. Yeah, most of us felt sad at his passing, I mean, come on, brain cancer, how horrible can it get?

Nevertheless, you really do not know what it is like until it hits you personally, and then you would not wish it on your worst enemy. The grief that usually follows the loss of a loved one, human or animal, can be debilitating. But the suffering that can also coincide with grief is completely self-induced. We have the power to reduce or eliminate our own suffering.

Loss and Grief

We created the Universe to experience love and joy on a level of contrast. In doing so, we dove into this physical experience with the conviction of a carpenter bee. However, we may not have realized that many facets to contrasting love and joy are extreme pain, including sadness, sorrow, and grief. Much to the same degree and capacity of love we can experience can we also experience sadness from loss. It is the yin and yang of emotion, much like a pendulum, and we must see it through to its full swing. We so wanted a physical world of contrast but were perhaps not prepared for what that might look like. Or perhaps as Creators we did understand the extremes and consequences of physical creation but concluded that to be human we must experience the pain that may be experienced by it.

Many cultures believe that we must experience pain as a consequence of our humanity. At the same time, there are some who are able to eliminate pain by disassociating mind from body through meditation and other practices of transcendental disconnection. There are also many who believe that this is the key to enlightenment of our true nature and only through such disconnection can this be achieved. I find it compelling that in order to find our true (real) natures we must be able to disconnect from the physical, which also lends credence to the physical reality we find ourselves as not being real in the first place. But as we live and breathe, loss seems quite real and painful and, at times, unimaginable.

Not until I lost the love of my life, Buddy, could I even begin to comprehend the terrible loss that Joe Biden and his family must have felt at the passing of Beau Biden and are undoubtedly still feeling today. You never get over the loss of a loved one. I have had family members make their transition from this physical world. Naturally, I had my brief moments of grief, but this was something completely different. When you bond with someone so closely, so perfectly, there is an underlying spiritual connection that is unbreakable and, I believe, eternal. Even though my recent loss was my dog, Buddy was more than a dog to me; he had been my closest companion for the past eleven years. I can honestly say I now know what it feels like to have lost such a strong physical bond and that spiritual connection. In an instant, his sudden departure made my world feel empty and less important. I felt lost without him, as if my emotional GPS had been removed. I felt as though a part of my life had been taken when his life was gone. His loss had me feeling as though my life was less important, had less meaning. That is how powerful our Ego's pull has upon own sense of reality, made to feel as though we have been robbed because of the identity we make with such loved ones.

The grief that resulted from that loss was gut-wrenching for many weeks and at times unimaginable. I wasn't sure how I was going to get over it, nor was I even sure I wanted to. I felt as if a hole had been cut out of my heart. Depression set in; at times I could hardly breathe. At times, I did not want to breathe and had to remind myself to breathe, to keep on going. I can understand how some people might contemplate suicide after such loss. After all, he was my world, and he had been taken from me before I was ready, seemingly in an instant. Now my world was completely shattered and empty. He had been fine one minute and gone the next. I wasn't ready!

All too often we develop a sense of anger from the sudden loss of a loved one. Our Ego does a great job of convincing us that it is our fault somehow, that we could have done something different to change the outcome. We fall into the guilt phase of thinking we should have done this or that, and it would be different if we had just done something differently. Before we realize how ridiculous this is, we can develop a deep depression over it that winds up to be much more drama than it deserves. We certainly feel hurt. When we do not know better, we get angry with God for allowing it to happen in the first place.

Understand that we would have no need to get angry with God, or anyone else for that matter, as this only adds to the negativity that can ultimately result in uncontrolled drama about it. It is important to remember that we cannot change what is because it has already happened. What happens in life cannot be reversed, no matter how much blame or guilt we place upon it. When we understand this, we can prevent or stop the drama from unfolding that adds to the pain we are already suffering from. When we understand that what we had was always temporary anyway, we can conclude that it was never really ours to begin with. When we stop making the loss about us, we can ease the pain and quicken its elimination.

When you live alone, such loss is even more devastating. Unlike some who have other family members around for solace and comfort, I had no one close by. I had no one to comfort me. Sure, friends would call on the phone, but sometimes one does not want to talk or even answer the phone. I can understand that now, even with family and friends close by. No other animal or human being can fill the void left behind. It seems that the physical bond is unique and irreplaceable, making acceptance of their departure all the more difficult.

It turns out that Buddy, like Beau Biden, also had cancer—pancreatic cancer. The vets could not say why or how, but we knew he was doomed the moment his liver enzymes showed that the cancer had already spread to his liver. There was no treatment. Days later, he was gone.

Buddy was a pure angel in my eyes, the love of my life, and it surely seemed like he was taken from me, out of my life, seemingly in an instant. I was not prepared, and even if I had been, I do not know if the grief would have been any easier to handle. Even though Buddy was only a dog, what that experience taught me is just how vested we can become in this physical world, especially with those who affect us the most. We become so vested that we can become ill when we are robbed of their touch, their smile, their unconditional love, and in Vice President Biden's case, I would imagine, a son's unwavering love and counsel. I understand such a close relationship and can tell you from firsthand experience that I trust no other human as I trust my own son, Matt. It is an exceptional bond. I have become so emotionally attached to him that the mere thought of permanent separation is almost too difficult to bear.

Why should we get so vested? Why should we be allowed to suffer so? I think it is because we lose lines of distinction, those lines that cross over into the world of another being. The more time we spend loving, the more those lines that separate us become blurred and completely overlapping. Our Egos have a way of binding us to others, sometimes to the unhealthy point of living their lives for them. As parents, we do this while raising our children and believe it is a part of good parenting. I call it the father-knows-best complex. We believe our decisions for others are done with good intentions. My belief is that we really do this because we become melded with another being to the point that we honestly believe that we are making decisions for ourselves. At times we become their lives and we can lose our own identities!

It is for this reason that the sudden loss of a loved one can be so physically painful, because we become so melded with that pet or that person that a part of us also dies with their passing. Walking around half dead is no fun. Depression can be completely debilitating, and the emotional pain can be as draining as physical pain. Our minds, at times, cannot differentiate between suffering emotionally and suffering physically. Losing a part of your soul is like losing a limb.

Overcoming the loss of a loved one can oftentimes be accomplished by complete preoccupation with either another person or another new pet. However, this may take some time. We must be able to put the grief behind us. To do that, we must not be afraid to face our feelings and allow our emotions to express themselves. Crying can be as healing for one as hard physical work can be for another. Whether you become depressed or just angry, you must be able to vent and express it. Just like a wound that becomes infected, the infectious nature of guilt and anger must be expressed out of us as well, or it will fester into an unhealthy mental, and ultimately a harmful physical, condition.

While I am not a psychotherapist, I say it is okay to stay in bed for a while, because if you are sleeping, you are not obsessing, and if you are not obsessing, you are not creating more drama about it. If you are not creating more drama about it, then you are not adding to your pain. In addition, since grief can be physically draining, rest seems to be a good option, if only temporary. However, it is of paramount importance that you stay healthy. You must keep eating and keep hydrated. Stock up on healthy snack foods and items that do not have to be cooked or at least can be quickly microwaved. Keep lots of fruit juices and smoothie mixes in the fridge. Take in some nourishment and then go back to bed for a while longer. Have bottled water by your bedside as well, so you can stay hydrated. Rest is good therapy, because grief can be very exhausting. Again, do not forget to eat! You cannot heal yourself if you become weak and useless. Remember: your departed loved one would not want his or her passing to cause you physical harm. You must honor their memories by staying healthy and strong.

Rest is good, but do not stay in bed for too long. Get out for a walk or sit in a darkened room and meditate. Remember, you cannot change what happened so do not obsess over the loss. Find solace in your spiritual world if you cannot find it in your physical world. If you can exercise, all the better. If a friend calls and offers you help, let him or her come over and do your dishes or laundry; the visit will do you good, and the friend will be happy to lend a hand with chores you are not up to performing yourself. If you do not have a friend who can help, hire someone to come in and clean. It's harder to get through depression if you end up living in a filthy mess. It is important for you to get back to something called "normal" as quickly as possible. Work (your job) can be a good distraction, but that will only occupy one third of your day. You must find other beneficial ways to fill in the rest of your waking hours. Perhaps starting a new hobby would fill the void.

Finally, allowing yourself time to grieve is vital. There is no time limit, so try to avoid the influence of others telling you how you should feel. You have a wonderful built-in guidance counselor within yourself; use it! There are also countless books on grief that may help you as well; use the experience of others to help you get through the nightmare. Trust that you can take care of yourself, as your departed loved one would want for you. Remember: the loved one would not wish for you to suffer or get ill from his or her loss, so get over it, for your loved one's sake. You can control that by not creating more drama about the entire situation. If you feel yourself slipping into despair, look in the mirror and tell yourself, "Get a grip!" If your depression should last longer than a week, I would advise you to get counseling from a professional bereavement counselor. Lastly, crying on someone's shoulder can also be therapeutic; that's what true friends are for. Getting emotional can be a good release of grief so it is important not to hold it in.

Suffering

Of course, there are varying degrees of suffering. Many believe that suffering plays an important role in a number of religions. For example, suffering is greatly defined in Buddhism and holds a key role in attaining the supreme bliss, enlightenment, or nirvana. Similarly, Hinduism holds that suffering follows naturally from personal negative behaviors in one's current life or in a past life (karma). Christianity also believes that human suffering plays an important role in religion. However, in Christianity, suffering is only thought to be a positive experience in the case of achieving a higher meaning of life, such as Jesus's suffering for the lives of others.

Many religions realize a need for God, as well as the moral significance for God that suffering provides. In Islam, the faithful must endure suffering with hope and faith, not resisting or asking why, accepting it as Allah's will and submitting to it as a test of faith (Allah never asks more than can be endured).[32]

Regardless of faith or religion, it seems that suffering is an integral part of our physical experience on Earth, but we do have control over the degree to which suffering can take place in our lives. The degree to which we suffer is equivalent to the drama we allow to compensate for the pain that is causing the suffering. Understand that can be either physical pain, mental pain, or both.

What I realize now is that we can either accept suffering in whatever form it comes (loving what is) or endure more of the same and keep the pain alive. We do have a choice. Change your mind about it; flip it to a positive advantage. Use the challenge in the direction of good.

Detachment and Letting Go

I have also realized our pain from loss can be mitigated if we have time to process the transition. While it is terrible to watch a loved one die a slow death, at least one has time to process the inevitable and begin our physical detachment; we can say our goodbyes. When we have time to process the truth of what is happening, we realize we are not *that* person or *that* pet, one with love in spirit, yes, but not one with their bodies. When we let go of that thought that we are a part of them physically, we begin the healing process before much suffering can take place. Remember: most of our suffering that stems from loss is due to our inability to let go. That is why drama about the loss takes shape. In many cases, we project the illness or pain onto ourselves as a possible coping mechanism. The physical connections we have with those we love are very strong, and our Ego requires a strong response. We feel the pain of losing them as if we were the one about to make the transition. The pain or drama we create from the loss somehow validates our love for that person (or animal). This is a false validation, however.

A famous colloquialism I learned from the Unity movement is "let go and let God." What this says to me is this: let go of those things that do not serve you, including anything that causes suffering, and replace it with something that does serve you. This makes sense because of our need to feel whole. When a piece of us is removed, it must be replaced, understanding that this is only a physical replacement, as the spiritual connections we have are never lost and can never die.

Eventually, what made it somewhat easier for me was realizing that Buddy was now in a far better place, free of pain. I envision him waiting for me, perhaps playing at the Rainbow Bridge[33] where we will be reunited one day. This brings me peace and comfort. My mental anguish over losing him was eventually outweighed by the physical pain he had been suffering as he developed the cancer that took over his little body. It almost feels selfish, in retrospect, to think that I could have kept him around a little longer, all while his body was being eaten away by cancer. I can now understand the difficulty we have when it is actually a close friend or family member, perhaps seeing him or her on life support, just so we can have him or her with us for one more day. Letting go of the physical attachment to Buddy, while extremely difficult, was a healing process in and of itself. I have since replaced that pain of letting go with joyous memories of how blessed I was to have him for all the years I did. Instead of feeling robbed by him being taken from me, I feel gifted to have had all his love in the first place. It is indeed better to have loved and lost than to never have loved at all, as they say. Now I am fed by the love, not the grief.

To the larger lesson that transcends loss and grief, it is important to detach from the physical investment that we make in other life-forms. It may be easier said than done, but if we try not to invest so heavily while such loved ones are alive, it will be easier to detach when their bodies surrender to age or illness. It is not necessary to love them less in order to achieve this. All we need to do is understand that it is not their physical bodies that we are attracted to, and realize that it is their spiritual essences that binds us. Only then, can we find it easier to detach without pain and suffering once their physical energy is taken from us. Understand and have faith that we will be reunited in the nonphysical realm, once we too have shed our physical bonds.

All we need to do is live in loving memory.

CHAPTER 7

What if there is enough resources to go around for everyone?

Our Perceived Need for Greed

You might have thought that if we spiritual beings created this world of abundance, greed would not be necessary. But there are consequences to a world built around laws of contrast. Like the Yin and Yang of emotion as mentioned earlier, our world of contrast is a world of the haves and have nots. It doesn't seem fair but it is all around us as perhaps a reminder of what we had created. We have good and bad, strong and weak, rich and poor. We cannot escape this reality, as they are the laws of contrast. Remember, before creating this world of contrast, all we wanted was to understand joy and love. We were naïve in our understanding of what would be required to accomplish this and that contrast would require the opposite of those things we sought to understand. A world of contrast is a world of comparison. To understand joy contrast requires misery. To understand love contrast requires hatred. To understand contentment contrast requires there to be fear and anxiety. The challenge for humans is being able to reconcile the extremes and choose which to identify with.

Greed is defined by Google as an intense and selfish desire for something, especially wealth, power, or food. It is thought that greed is a personality flaw. Thom Hartmann goes even further to outline greed as a psychological disorder[34]. Then what is at the heart of greed, and why are many human beings convinced for the need of greed to survive?

I believe that Greed is a result of a misconception that there is not enough to go around. But it goes beyond a personal desire to survive or succeed. You can see greed in many societies, and many institutions. Many corporations have become greedy in their desire to make a profit and keep their shareholders satisfied, most often at the expense of their consumers with higher prices. But the strategy I see in corporations today is the greedy desire to gain the most market share in an attempt put their competitors out of business. It had gotten so bad in the United States that U.S. Congress enacted laws limiting conglomerates and monopolies. One might argue such laws have only had limited success because where there is greed there is money and money has the power to persuade and influence the very laws trying to curtail them.

Greed and Nepotism

Certain societies can be seen to keep commerce within their own sects, thereby prospering their own kind, their own people, at the expense of their neighbors. Nepotism goes even further by limiting who you gave employment to. It was understood it better to give the work to a relative than a stranger because that relative can keep the money flowing within the family. In the early days of mankind, tribes would often limit trade within the tribe, keep trade more of a barter system. But as they became productive in producing goods and services, they actually found it beneficial to trade outside the tribe and hence began the expansionism of trade that we see today, and eventually created our global economy. Yet, greed still exists today and nepotism is alive and well. Why?

Greed and Scarcity

We have been programmed to believe that it is necessary to be greedy in order to survive. From the earliest time of our existence, we were taught carnal fortitude to succeed in life. We understood the belief that only the strong survive, to each his own, and that this is a catch-as-catch-can world. Well, maybe this was the case when mastodons ruled the Earth, but it is not true today.

Greed is reinforced with the false premise of scarcity, that there is not enough to go around. So you better stake your claim, come Hell or high water, or you will be left in the cold to perish! We have also been taught survival of the fittest in order to stake our claim. This is always the argument or justification for our greed. At times, our Id personalities are behind our reactions to scarcity, and greed is always the result.

It is this idea of scarcity that gives us the justification that what we do for protection in life is, of course, righteous and warranted. During more primeval times, there was a belief that a man would lose standing in his community if he could not show that he could conquer and secure dominion over things, such as women, land, and other resources like food, shelter, and water. Early humans must have had the idea of a do-or-die mentality from the thought of scarcity and there not being enough to go around. In our recent history, it seems to have become the game of "he who dies with the most wins!" Regardless of the reasons, it seems that we can label the need for greed as purely selfish and false, because there is enough—there is plenty to go around.

It is important to reiterate that greed goes hand in hand with the idea of scarcity. However, the fear of scarcity was not the only means used to justify greed. The idea of having more than your neighbor meant that you had more power. More power in society meant that you had a larger say at the table of influence in society. Often, being greedy was synonymous for being a power-monger. The more power you had, the less likely you were to being overruled.

Successful people are oftentimes viewed as wicked and greedy when their success comes without benevolence. If humans were instead encouraged at an early age to understand that there is enough to go around, there would be little need for greed or hording and, hence, no need for scavenging. I hazard to guess there would be a lot less cause to feud, squabble, or declare war against each other, if we really understood this principle. And that principle is universal; a life-force of abundance which awaits each of us. It is a stream of well-being that we can tap into at any time. The beautiful thing about it is there is no limit, and because there is no limit, it matters not how many souls take advantage of this stream. There is enough well-being to go around for everyone.

Greed relies on, and is justified by, the lie that there is not enough to go around. And so this creates a need for hording and depriving others of what we seek to attain, but it does not have to be. Those who are in a weaker position in life are probably predestined to miss out, or at least have things kept from them, because they have also bought into the lie that there is not enough to go around. And those who believe in scarcity will do everything to not only survive but to abscond with everything they can in order to ensure their survival long-term, even if it means taking more than their fair share. When greed is caused by fear, it creates amnesia, and we forget our love for one another. Our survival instinct takes over, and compassion is easily forsaken.

Greed and Slavery

We have witnessed slavery of all kinds throughout history. Even in this day and age, we can be slaves to fashion, slaves to technology, slaves to religion, slaves to injustice, and of course to our detriment, slaves to substance abuse. But these are all psychological forms of slavery. The most seemingly hideous kind of slavery of all has to be that of human slavery, dating back thousands of years.

According to Wikipedia,

> Slavery can be traced back to the earliest of recorded history (c. 1860 BC), which refers to it as an established institution, and it was common among ancient peoples.[35]

Today, Americans are constantly reminded of the original sin of slavery in the United States, not just by our history books where slavery is well documented, but by many social groups who feel that enslavement continues in other ways, transmuted into racial discrimination, racial profiling, human trafficking, and other social injustices. It always seems to circle back to "way back when" our ancestors traded people as commodities, treating certain groups with very little human dignity.

Some would argue that there may have been a quid pro quo, and in some cases this may be true. For some, you could have been "hired" as a slave to do work on a plantation, for example, and been given land and a home to occupy in exchange. However, this light form of encumbrance was not the norm. For most, human slavery was a torturous aspect of living, existing in fear, pain, and misery. Any civilized society should view human slavery as an abomination of our humanity in the highest degree, falling just short of terrorism and genocide.

Sadly, still today, slavery is alive and well, in the form of human trafficking. According to an article found at the HuffingtonPost.com,

> *"Trafficking in persons has become a big business. Globally, it's a $32 billion industry involving 161 countries — including the United States. Trafficking in persons involves activities where one person obtains or holds another person in compelled service. While many people are aware of sex trafficking, human trafficking that involves forced labor is far more prevalent. Some 78 percent of forced labor is based on state- or privately-imposed exploitation, not forced sexual exploitation."*[36]

This is precisely my point - human slavery has always been about greed. Wealthy landowners used slaves to do the hot, back-breaking work that most white men would not do unless paid handsomely. Such landowners believe they could not make a high enough profit unless they could get such labor done for only the cost of room and board. And so they bought, and sold, other human beings as personal property to do this work instead. Today, we allow migrant workers, some illegal, to travel here to do this work, but they are at least paid for their sweat, albeit at an illegal and most always below U.S. minimum wages. And of course the only difference is that they come willingly here to work, but still, they may feel that they have no choice.

Ironically, while slavery was finally abolished in the United States in 1865 by the Thirteenth Amendment to our Constitution, greedy corporations in the United States and around the world still look the other way while exporting the manufacturing of their goods to countries that used forced or slave labor. In fact, the Global Slavery Index reports that in 2016, it is estimated that 45.8 million people are in some form of modern slavery in 167 countries[37].

What right does anyone believe that they have over another human being to the degree that they can buy, sell, or trade them? Should the greed of money be enough to convey such rights to buy or sell another human being? Should parents have the right to sell their children into perpetual servitude? Amazingly, there are still cultures out in the world today that believe in this greedy and selfish act, perhaps steeped in tradition that has been handed down for generations. Still, we must not lose the significance of it for the sake of tradition. The question is, will the greed of slavery ever end?

Greed and Martyrdom

Recently, I reflected on the concept of martyrdom and have concluded that it is not out of sacrifice that people opt to become martyrs; it is purely out of selfishness and greed. When thinking about suicide bombers, for example, it seems to such people that there is no way out (of a particular negative situation or circumstance) and that a greedy act of violence in some way justifies their need to get out a message on the negativity or injustice that they are attempting to highlight. Their rage may be fueled by a severe thought or a feeling of powerlessness. But it is purely out of selfishness and greed for them that they believe that martyrdom will give them back their power. What they fail to realize is that their greedy act is an assault and a personal loss to not only the family and friends of the victims, but also to the innocent family and friends of the martyr himself or herself. Somehow, the power that greed has over them has them convinced that their act is justified and righteous. I think historians will conclude that martyrs succeed at nothing except more negativity, death, and destruction. They are not helping their cause; they only compound and magnify the injustices that they seek to draw attention to. They do not understand the power of attraction. They are only adding fuel to an already senseless fire. They are making their situation worse, not to mention, adding more misery to their own families and communities in the wake of their acts of violence.

Unfortunately, violence can only promote more of the same. It is a universal law of attraction—like begets like. There is nothing good or useful that an act of violence can offer a society or the world. Thinking differently and not buying into the lie takes an act of courage. The tragedy is in the lie that martyrs believe in, that their violent act will somehow make a positive difference in their community and in the world, and that they will be rewarded for their act of selflessness in the next life or afterlife. It is not an act of selflessness, however. It is an act of selfishness, and selfishness in this regard is surely another word for greed.

I think in the case of martyrs, the frustration of not being heard is where a mentality of greed begins to fester. Again, it is caused by a feeling of powerlessness, and Ego provides the lack and limitation case to justify a course of action and retaliation. At this point "dis-ease" (uneasiness, anxiety, and frustration) turns to disease, a disease in the mind of a normally rational thinker. The only cure that I can see for this disease is love and understanding. Unfortunately, it seems that there are plenty of very influential members of their society who do not believe in, or subscribe to, love and understanding. In some cases, their elders preach martyrdom in order to help demonstrate and magnify their own injustices. What if they have an old axe of their own to grind, and they use their youth as pawns, one could even say slaves to injustice?

Ego is first in line to help confirm that such greed is a necessary evil. It convinces us that we have an individual right to trump the status quo with violence at the expense of reason and sanity and, surely, at the expense of love for one another. Of course, the true irony is that it requires so much more effort to curse and hate someone than it does to love them. It takes much more energy to hurt someone, than to help them or forgive them. According to Snopes.com, *"It takes 37 muscles to frown. And 22 muscles to smile. So Smile. It conserves energy) :) :)."*[38] The point is, anger, hate, violence, and martyrdom serve very little purpose, take much more energy, and do not provide a positive solution to that for which they are trying to highlight.

Greed, Consumptionism, and the Destruction of Family

During Pope Francis's recent visit to the United States, in one of his last lectures given to the global bishops in Philadelphia, the pontiff reminded us that self-protection is a product of "consumptionism" and is contrary to family, contrary to neighborly love, and above all, contrary to trust. Pope Francis said that today's culture does not encourage bonds of trust. He also went on to say that family is a blessing from God and that we must get back to a simple truth, that family must reign supreme. In that speech, he urged the bishops of the Catholic Church to make family, once again, their top priority! It was a beautiful and poignant speech and it really touched on the essence of further reconciliation within the church.

I think it is true that greed does indeed create an atmosphere of mistrust and certainly has the power to divide us. It has us creating silos of exclusionism, where we hide out and escape the evidence of our gluttony. This separates us further, and therefore, I must conclude that greed is the antithesis of family and community.

In Hillary Clinton's book, *It Takes a Village*, I believe her use of the word *village* includes the idea of community and family in society. It is therefore quite possible that the issues facing our youth today could be directly related to the breakdown of family and society. Greed has us ignore our true calling to one another, to help one another, to protect and love one another. Earlier, I related how engaging my conversations were with my uncle Jack. I also identified that my general aptitude for learning may have a lot to do with this form of mental stimulation. When I see how our society has progressed with both parents working full-time jobs, it is clear that a lot less time remains for having stimulating conversations with our children. That is when aunts and uncles, sisters and brothers, can step up to help.

I believe that Hillary was attempting to convey that we owe it to each other, especially to our children, to be there to fill in when gaps in society role models occur. Such gaps take place when a father or mother or older sibling or other family elder leaves the home, whether temporarily for hunting for food or for long distance travel for work, or more permanently due to death, divorce, or moving to another area for school, work, or marriage. There really is not much difference in the early times of the hunter-gatherer, when men had to leave the village for days on end to hunt for game to feed the village, and women had to also gather what they could to survive in the meantime. At some point, we learned that greed was not the answer—neighbor helping neighbor was the answer. Most tight-knit societies were one big family. Scarcity was not as pressing on individuals because there was a common purpose; they put unity in community. Don't we still owe that to each other? Doesn't our neighbor deserve help and assistance in his or her times of need, even if just to help a child with schoolwork? Can't we be there for others' children as they may do for ours?

I find it ironic that while physically our houses are built closer and closer together, the neighborhoods we live in seem to be split emotionally further and further apart. I wonder how many people actually speak to their neighbors on a regular basis or even know their names? I am guilty as charged and at times feel ambiguous about it. I stay to myself, I don't bother anyone, and they don't bother me, so why should I get involved, why be that nosey neighbor? I think I was raised that way. But it sure seems lonely to some degree when you do not concern yourself with others right next door.

It seems unconscionable for the elderly to live alone without family and friends looking out for them and also neighbors who do not look in on them. It feels shameful when one thinks about it. What happened to the days when a young start-up family moved in and the community gathered for an entire weekend to help them build a barn so that they could raise their own farm animals and gain a level footing? Of course, that's just an example, because most of us no longer require raising farm animals to survive. But you get my point. We need to come together again as a family, in the human family, putting commune and unity back into community.

Deepak Chopra said,

> *Right this moment there's a huge economic crisis, an economic meltdown, there's global warming, there's wars, there's terrorism, there is social injustice, and there's a world where 50% of the world lives on $2 per day, and of that half, lives on less than $1 a day. The situation couldn't be worse. This is a moment of chaos and crisis. But in the proliferation of that crisis is the opportunity for a creative leap and we are now willing, I hope, to take that leap, where we don't confuse money with wealth. Money is the symbolic expression for what we give importance to, so money is right now a Wall Street casino. 2.9 trillion dollars circulates in the world's markets every day, of that less than 2% goes to provide goods and services to the world. So 98% and more is speculation and debt. There's no money, there's only debt! So we are buying things with money that we have not earned, [to] buying things that we don't need with money that we haven't earned to impress people that we don't like. And now we're saying we can't do that anymore so we're unhappy. We have to replace the idea of money with wealth. Wealth is the*

progressive realizing of worthy goals, wealth is the ability to love and have compassion, wealth is good health, wealth is caring relationships, and wealth is getting in touch with the creative source inside you, which is also the creative source of the whole Universe of space time energy information and matter. When we shift from money to wealth we will have found the Kingdom of Heaven which is in us."[39]

Dr. Chopra makes a clear distinction between having tangible assets (money) and less tangible assets (wealth). Sharing our wealth does not have to cost us money and may only cost us a little love, compassion, and devotion (time). I am sure you can agree, as we shift to this new mind-set of wealth, we will be much more content, and the world will be a better place. And, there will be less need for greed.

Selfishness

Most of us do not offer to help our neighbors because we are programmed to believe in reciprocity, and this leads to selfishness. Yet we are taught at an early age that being selfish is analogous to being greedy and that the act of being selfish is wrong. We are also taught that selfishness lacks consideration for others, because it deprives someone else of something you have that you may be able to contribute in some way.

A wiki definition of selfishness is,

"Being concerned, sometimes excessively or exclusively, for oneself or one's own advantage, pleasure, or welfare, regardless of others."[40]

That definition may hold true when carried out by our Id personality, because it is more closely related to our survival mechanism. However, when carried out by the Ego, the definition takes on a whole other meaning. When you think, *It looks like Joe could use a hand lifting those boxes into his truck*, and then think, *Yeah, well, he never helps me when I need help, so I think I'll ignore him*, that is selfishness on the level of Ego that maintains a what's-in-it-for-me attitude. Again, when Ego interjects in our decision-making, there is usually no sense of community. Selfishness on this level is at the expense of others and brings on a negative energy with it. I think that when we can make most of our decisions based upon being of service to others without the "what's-in-it-for-me" attitude, we will find our connection to God is much stronger.

I would not characterize selfishness as necessarily being a bad attribute unless it is at the expense of someone else. There are plenty of exceptions to selfishness being beneficial. Take, for example, when you are on an airplane. One of the first safety awareness exercises performed by cabin crew is to instruct you in being selfish in order to be able to assist others later. They will tell you before each and every flight, "In case there is a loss in cabin pressure, yellow oxygen masks will deploy from the ceiling compartment located above you. Please make sure to secure your own mask first before assisting others." The reason for this instruction is not always obvious to some people. The answer is, of course, that when you are normally in the care of another person, like a child or senior citizen, you will be of no assistance to him or her if you passed out while trying to secure their masks first. It may be too late for them to help themselves without your aid, so it is important that you maintain your full faculties in order to aid someone else. I am sure this act of selfish kindness has been studied enough to be standard operating procedure on airlines for good reason.

Also, in order to be good and kind to others, you must be good and kind to yourself first. For without clarity of mind, there would be little for you to offer anyone else. Loving oneself and putting yourself first is not really about being selfish at all. Going within and finding clarity with who you really are, before all others, will enable you to love others more fully and without judgments or preconditions. If you cannot experience love and compassion first hand with yourself, how can you extend it to someone else?

Abraham-Hicks makes a good argument for being selfish by saying you cannot lead from behind! I wish to emphasize that it does not mean depriving anyone of anything they already have access to! We can be empowered through the abundance of Source Energy. We created the Universe of Source Energy for a reason—to tap into it anytime we choose! So why aren't we tapping into it all the time? What if it is because we are still not aware that this is a limitless resource? We simply need to change our minds about lack, and focus not upon limitations, but instead upon the abundance that we so richly deserve.

Arrogance

Arrogance is one way that Ego defends our greed, but it is another silent killer. It proves, repeatedly, that it can and will turn against us and even lead to tragedy. Martyrdom is a good example of this combination of greed and arrogance. Even at the most benign level, arrogance is a cancer on our innocence and leads us to greed, destruction, and war.

I have often pondered why this should be so. Could it be that arrogance ignores our blessings and forces us to believe that we are especially deserving and that we belong? When we believe that we are self-deserving at all costs, greed is then instantly justified. Arrogance can cause irrational thinking. It creates a bubble in which sane thoughts cannot enter. We become invincible, and we believe that we are that super-hero that no one can touch. This transcends the power of positive thinking. It is pure arrogance, a Teflon coating that shields us from any resistance to our actions. We are masters of the Universe and should not be questioned or harmed. Can you think of anyone who ran for the highest office in the land that fits that description?

I think that a little humility goes a long way. Instead of being arrogant in assuming we have it all or deserve it all or know it all, perhaps we should replace that line of thinking with the understanding that we are blessed just the way we are, endowed with all we need in this moment. We do not require substantiation by the Ego or otherwise. Arrogance leads us to assume, and we know where that can lead. Don Miguel Ruiz's third agreement states, "**Don't Make Assumptions**!" It goes on to say, "Find the courage to ask questions and to express what you really want. Communicate with others as clearly as you can to avoid misunderstandings, sadness and drama."[41] Adhering to this agreement will help to eliminate arrogance in our lives.

Sounds like common sense, doesn't it? So then why is it that we see so many people who assume they know everything? I think there is a hidden truth in that agreement, in finding the courage to ask questions, for not doing so makes us cowards. But we do not see it that way because Ego has us believing we know it all. Why do we assume we know that so-and-so is talking about us in a negative light, without having heard a word of what he or she might have said? Without asking for clarification on what we think we know about, or what we think we heard from someone, we are being arrogant. Once again, arrogance leads to assumptions that are usually not founded in facts and are often times wrong. What results is a lot of drama that usually comes from nothing substantial. Remember: the Ego loves drama so that is why, with Ego's help, we fall victim to assumptions.

While we are indeed worthy of all that is good, we should not believe that goodness is limited, and we should understand that there is enough to go around. There are plenty of brilliant people in the world who claim there is plenty for each of us, more than we need actually. They believe that not one person in the world should have to go hungry or die from starvation or be deprived of clean drinking water. And this should be our paramount act—conservation of the scarcer resource of fresh, clean water, as it is predicted that the deprivation of fresh, clean drinking water may lead to the next war of the haves and have-nots. I predict our next world war may be over fresh, clean drinking water and not oil, so we must do all that we can to act now to prevent this.

But this again leads arrogance back to greed, and the greed of water usage in agriculture is a good example. We are still farming crops that require vast amounts of water, instead of growing more crops that are drought resistant. And while people are actually dying from lack of clean drinking water in the world, we see rich places in Nevada that waste trillions of gallons of water each year simply to water lawns! Why? Because they can, and because they have the money to throw away, and this leads us back to arrogance and greed!

It doesn't have to be this way. We can conserve so there is more to share for our current and future generations. We simply need to be more conscious of our actions. There is more than enough to go around if we would only reduce or eliminate our greedy behaviors.

CHAPTER 8

What if we are just naïve little lambs?

I speak of politics and religion to highlight certain inequities that seem to fuel much of the division in our great nation. When it comes to our politics, many Americans like to frame parts of the U.S. Constitution around their own ideologies, often to the chagrin of their neighbors. Some interpretations have fueled civil unrest, especially when it comes to the Right to Bear Arms. And notions of a new Civil War within our country have fear circulating amongst peace-loving citizens. The same can be said of religion when it comes to interpreting our ancient religious texts. Oftentimes, people take such ancient words very literally, having no real world understanding, or proof, of what the authors really intended way back when. Like some interpretations of the U.S. Constitution, many interpretations of the Judeo Christian Bibles have me quite perplexed. I will touch on both as they do affect my personal philosophy and much of this writing is based upon that.

However, one might be asking; what does all this have to do with ideas on Creation and our Universe? I suppose it is to illustrate that, soon after we created this world of contrast, we had to accept that there would be division. Because a world of contrast is a world of opposites, and that includes our personal ideas of right and wrong, legal and illegal, fair and unfair, good and evil. All of these 'contrasting' points of view confirm our physical world and so it should be understood that there will never be 100 percent agreement on anything. I sometimes offer suggestions in my way of trying to bridge the gaps, but some will probably not see it that way.

Separating Church and State

Except for Christianity, I cannot speak to other religions because I was born into a mostly Christian family and being raised in the United States I was easily subjected to more Christian doctrines than any other. So this is what I have been exposed to throughout my life. I speak of the separation of Church and State because our founding fathers did not want the two to mix. I supposed this was because, as a 'free people', we should have to right to choose any religion that we wish to practice (or not practice) and not to be dictated to, or influenced, by our government. The concept dates back to Thomas Jefferson's writing influence on the Virginia Statute for Religious Freedom. This important Commonwealth Statute ultimately influenced both the drafting of the First Amendment to the U.S. Constitution and the United States Supreme Court's understanding of religious freedom (according to encyclopediavirginia.org). However, the Separation of Church and State is not specifically written in the Bill of Rights, it is a philosophic and jurisprudential concept for defining political distance in the relationship between religious organizations and the state (according to wikipedia.org). The First Amendment to our Constitution is more broadly referred to as our "Freedom of Religion", and many Americans these days may even refer to it as our freedom "from" religion!

As I became an adult, it seemed that the Christian religions in our country were somewhat divisive, I mean, why was Christianity divided into so many denominations in the first place? There seemed to be very little cohesion between them in my mind, although they all, for the most part, centered upon Jesus Christ in the New Testament Bible.

I was not brought up religious as they say, far from it. Yet looking in from the outside, such divisions often confused me. I only remember going to church on Easter Sunday's. However, I was exposed to the Holy Bible[42] and other concepts of Christianity and God through friends and acquaintances. I was not a complete idiot to Christianity, but, I knew even less about other religions such as Islam, Hinduism or Buddhism. Therefore, I can only share my interpretations of Christianity for purposes of illustrating my conclusions about religion in general.

What concerned me was that the divisions in Christianity must come from unique and differing interpretations of the meanings in certain Holy Scriptures. So how could Christianity be divided into so many different groups, I wondered. Certainly, Catholics, Methodists and Protestants and Pentecostals and Episcopalians and Baptists and Mormons and Lutherans and Presbyterians, and on and on, must have some issues with what has been written regarding the Christian doctrines they were to adhere to. It must be understood that their differences were so absolute that they had to separate and create their own denomination. This troubled me, and it made me very suspicious about the Christian faith in general. How was I supposed to be a true Christian if I had to choose which denomination was "the correct one"? Do I study each denomination and then cherry-pick what more aligns with my way of thinking? Isn't this how they came to be? This concept was somewhat unsettling to me, but humans tend to cherry-pick most important issues so is seems logical that this has taken place through the ages.

Growing up, I found the Bible brimming with interesting and enlightening stories. Yet alas, little faith had I for taking the Bible at its word, for much of what I had read did not resonate absolute truth within me. Throughout my adolescence, I never really knew why. What I would later discover is that absolution would never come. Still, I tried to be a good little Christian. You know—doing and saying the "right" things.

I suppose the foremost reason for me not having absolute faith was that I struggled with the brashness of the Bible, most of which was portrayed as though God had penned the book Himself. To me this seemed almost arrogant and certainly illogical. It was perhaps in my early struggles to reason with things (like the writings in the Bible) that I later became a computer programmer by profession. It seemed second nature to me, dealing with logic by the time I reached adulthood. I loved digital logic because programming computers was absolute. At the core of all computers is a binary decision-making system using logic gates. Computers work by asking a series of questions, and decisions are based upon either true or false answers. There is nothing in between, there is nothing ambiguous, and there is no maybe.

Over the years I have grappled with the concept of not only the Bible's dictation, but also how many different people would have scribed the more than two dozen books in the Old Testament and the twenty-seven books in the New Testament, not to mention the dozens of hidden or forbidden non canonized books, including the Gospel of Mary Magdalene[43]. The thought that many ancient writings had been buried and hidden from us "little lambs" seemed so patronizing to me and to that of the public at large. Was there something in them that was so far off the mainstream that the so-called scholars of the day decided to eliminate them? What if it was out of fear of rebellion or anarchy?

I also wondered how many times the original text of the Bible and other various writings had been translated over the centuries and how embellished with prejudice and bias such writings may have received during translations and subsequent transcriptions. Such a huge influence and confluence of people setting such text to a readable medium was surely to have had an effect on its original dictation, and ultimately, I believe, has taken a toll on its authenticity. Let's not forget the simple childhood game called "telephone." Subject any topic to scores of people speaking and writing in different languages and what do you imagine you will end up with? It's anyone's guess. The end result is never the same as what began, just as with the childhood game proves.

As I matured and left my adolescence, my angst grew over a better understanding of the Bible, and I began to search for its authenticity. During my search, I also began to question my own purpose and role in the Universe, and whether or not I should even believe in a God. Some people, like my father, did not believe there was a God or a Heaven. So I wondered, could they be right? I have memories of conversations with my father about death before he made his transition in 1998. I like to call it a *transition* because I believe our life-forces can never be destroyed, only transitioned from one life-form to another. Once I made this determination, my belief is that we never really die; we only transition. But father had a different idea. He believed we simply cease to exist, and he intimated that any spirit we might have dies along with our physical bodies.

As with many scientists who cannot explain what was in the instance before the big bang, my father had his own conclusions that this was all there was. While I respected my father, who was quite intelligent despite not having a formal college education, this notion was certainly not logical in my mind. However, I was not sure why I felt that way back then. I was still in my search for truth. Little by little, with either logic or deep-seated heartfelt notions, I began to stitch together pieces of truth that resonated with me, and it has woven a tapestry of what I believe today.

It is certainly disheartening when I encounter people who take every word in such ancient texts so literally. So, it is not very surprising to me that societies are exposed to bigotry, intolerance, discrimination, and what appears to be an inability for people to think outside the box. Of course, our Egos would have our personal rendition of any biblical story to be the correct one, meaning, the translation from everyone else must be wrong! This gets back to the pitfalls of arrogance that I described earlier because it portrays the greed that "I alone know the truth!" Well let me just state for the record that I do not know the truth, nor do I have all the answers, and suspect that I will be searching for the truth until I make my transition from this life. And just to be clear, anyone that claims they have all the answers is living in a fantasy world. All I can do herein is share what makes logical sense to me, and explain to you the problems I have had in reasoning our certain topics such as religion and the doctrine they are founded upon.

Moreover, what comes out of many so-called Christian mouths goes against what Jesus the Christ was attempting to teach his followers in the day. Jesus paramount lesson for us was about love and compassion and especially forgiveness! For those who believe themselves to be good Christians (or good Muslims or good Hindus) who are professing notions contrary to love, compassion, and forgiveness, then how can you call yourself a good steward of your faith? How can you consider yourself to be a good Christian (Muslim or Hindu) if you support any form of hatred, violence, or bigotry? How can you profess yourself to be a good Christian (Muslim or Hindu) if you alienate people based upon their personal beliefs, regardless of whether those beliefs of religious and/or sexual preferences may differ from your own? Love and compassion dictate that it is not necessary for others to be like you in order for you to love them. If you believe yourself to be a good person, ask yourself, what would Jesus do (or what would Mohamed or the Bhagavad Gita subscribe to)? How would Jesus (or other revered avatars) behave or react in a given situation? If your goal is to be a good Christian (for example), wouldn't you wish to behave as Jesus would behave? If the answer is yes, then I suggest forgiving yourself for any transgressions you may have made against another human being. Forgive yourself for any prejudices or hatred you may have for others. Forgive yourself for judging others, for this will allow the love within you to flow forth freely and so that you may find yourself at peace. Living a life of forgiveness and reduced judgments will eliminate most drama in your life and allow you to live more joyfully.

Getting a different perspective later in life, I eventually understood what Jesus had to say. I could see how this line of thinking may have been perceived as outrageous; the people of that time were not prepared or ready for thinking such profound thoughts. The vast majority of common folk were not learned enough to comprehend ideas never considered before, never discussed before. Understand that only the very elite were allowed to study and learn to read during that time, so such stories and lessons were very hard to come by in written form. Most were handed down through storytelling around campfires and dinner tables. There were no court reporters taking down dictation back then. Even stories told of Jesus Christ had to be based upon memory, which could have been years later before they were transcribed. Therefore, scribing such stories were often secondhand at best, and most legal-minded people might go so far as to say it was "hearsay". Yet, you will find most people who preach the Bible refuse to treat any of it as hearsay. This, again, was illogical for me.

Politics

Politics seems eerily similar to religion in the sense that few seem to be in agreement, thus, politics has been as divided as some religions, it seems. I also grew up in a time of war and hatred, and I could see anger and ugliness in people all around me. I remember news reports of our war in Vietnam, and I could not make any sense of it. At an early age, I would learn of body bags and death on a massive scale. Even with my young naïve mind, I questioned; what were we doing halfway around the world, fighting in a country that did not even speak English? This did not make any sense to me. Why would our government send thousands of our young men into harm's way? What was the reason? What was the purpose? What were we fighting for? Moreover, how could a loving God allow so many deaths or allow wars to begin with?

When I was eight or nine years old, my young uncle, barely ten years older than me, was drafted to serve in the US Army, and I worried if I would ever see him again. Would he come home alive when the war in

Vietnam was finally over? Thankfully, he did come home. But before it ended, nearly fifty thousand US soldiers had lost their lives in combat in an ugly war that seemed completely and utterly pointless. When all was said and done, what did we gain? The same could be said for the 1950's Korean war. Look where we are today. What was gained?

I did not understand politics very well back then or the concept that a country would align with another country in order to assert its values and principles, politics, or better yet, its greedy economics. As for Vietnam, I would later ask my grandfather, why did we get involved in what seemed to be an internal civil war in a third-world country? And he would tell me, "To stop the spread of communism." To which I remember thinking, *Why? Why was it our job to stop the spread of communism?* Finally, he would just say in effect that we were there in order to protect democracy. Politicians would say it was for the national security of the United States. Yet, still confused, I would stop asking such questions and began a sense of distrust of most governments and their true intentions.

Nevertheless, personal chaos would also reside in Miami where I grew up. As an adolescent, I was surrounded by bigotry, discrimination, and racial strife, resulting in segregation and violence on every level, from name-calling to gang fighting. People just could not seem to get along. I saw rioting and many unreasonable deaths, when I was a young lad. It seems not much has changed fifty years later.

Why was I bullied by the black boys in my school and beat up in the stairwells for no reason? I remember thinking, *Why do they hate me? Just for being white?* I had not done anything wrong to anyone; I was innocent. "Can we all get along?"[44] Why were people so angry all the time?

It turns out that many people throughout the world have such ongoing fights with innocent people, as they hold on to deep-seated grudges for the past transgressions of others. What really makes no sense to me is carrying around that kind of hatred and animosity for so long and for reasons that are such old news. The weight of such baggage can only serve to hold a person back, in my mind. Certainly, this must be a burden, so why continue it?

Most wars would make little sense to me, especially the recent war in Iraq, fueled by such profound words as "axis of evil" and "weapons of mass destruction." Why would the spoken word be used so often to defame and degrade another human being or another country or society? The answer always comes down to **fear!**

While the United States offers the best constitution of governance and Bill of Rights for its people, we also have the right to argue and complain and to contradict it. We have been conditioned for instant gratification, instant success, and instant reward. That resulting greed can turn a perfect constitution into a dysfunctional and unfair state of governance, and I think we are seeing more of that reflected in our U.S. Congress today.

Of course, one could argue this is less about instant gratification and more about one party of governance trying to replace the other at all costs. Therefore, no state of affairs would be good enough. How have we become so divided? With the dysfunction in government becoming so evident, how can we complain without changing the source of the problem—our elected officials?

My take is that most of us are just plain spoiled. Even when we see improvements in a situation, it is never good enough, and a good politician can always swing your opinion by focusing on something undesirable to reinforce your negative feeling about it. We focus on the negative instead of the positive and then wonder why things are not improving fast enough. Ironically, the same people that expect the government to turn on a dime are the same people who do not believe in larger government involvement to begin with. In order to move forward though, don't we need to strike a balance between opposing ideas? What happened to honest accommodation? Have our Egos gotten so large that we are incapable of compromise? We must come together at some point as a nation, not a political party.

If the last decade or more of our US Congress are not proof enough of dysfunction, I don't know what is. The popular view of Congress, at this moment, is that many members are acting like a bunch of children, opposing one another in defiance just because they can, cutting off their noses to spite their faces. How shallow and childish do you have to be, for a sitting congressional representative to openly pronounce that he (or she) will do everything to obstruct the 44th president of the United States, just because he was elected by the opposite political party? Could this be a sign of bigotry in the highest degree? Or worse yet, since Obama is a person of color, could this be a sign that racism is alive and well in the 21ˢᵗ Century? Many Americans might answer, both.

If we are going to solve some of our biggest problems in this country, that kind of attitude must change. A concerted effort to accommodate might go a long way to stop usurping and dictating policy against the US electorates will. This may remain very difficult, as long as billions of dollars are allowed for lobbying, regardless of whether those ideas are in the people's best interest or not. Still, money talks. Therefore, we may need to outlaw lobbying of our elected representatives in order for honest compromise to take place with such financial influences. And we still have the issue of the unfairness when it comes to the U.S. Senate, where each State is only allowed two Senators, regardless of the population in which that State represents. With California having over 51 times the population of North Dakota and yet only granted the same 2 Senate representatives, you can see how our politics gets very infuriating for many Americans.

Despite the inequities in our politics, I continue to be optimistic for the survival of our Republic. So the choice is ours; to either focus on and magnify what is working for us (our positive energies), or to focus on and magnify that which is not working for us (our negative energies). You can guess what my choice has been. Now, if Congress could only do the same.

When it comes to fair elections in our country, there are two issues the U.S. Congress should vote to permanently change. The first item would be to make gerrymandering illegal. This would go a long way to help ensure a fair representation for the people in congress, as many congressional districts throughout the U.S. have been very unfairly and arbitrarily drawn. The second item would be to abolish the Electoral College system in the election of our U.S. President. This would go a long way to help ensure a fair election for the highest office in the land. Because of the antiquated Electoral College system, Democrats have been wronged twice in recent years due to electing a Republican president when it was clear that a majority of Americans (the popular vote) voted otherwise. So in the eyes of Democrats, Bush and Trump were both elected against the will of the people. This is not what democratically held elections should be about. Regardless of party affiliation, the majority, or "popular" vote, should decide the presidency in our modern age.

God and Religion

As I began to question the reality around me, it was natural to question God and His role in all the chaos in our world. How could there be a God, who was/is portrayed as almighty and all-powerful, sitting idly by and allowing such violence and injustice? In addition, what about all the natural disasters that He would "allow," such as tornadoes, floods, volcanic eruptions, hurricanes, earthquakes and wildfires? Oftentimes these disasters wipe out hundreds, even thousands, of innocent lives in horrible and grotesque ways. Was this the all-loving God I was supposed to worship and believe in? So Dad was on to something when he contended that God did not exist, for it seems quite illogical and contradictory for an all-loving God to be part of this madness.

Things would eventually settle in my mind about God and religion. After I turned forty years of age, I embarked upon a more spiritual path. After moving back to Miami, I made my home next to a Unity church. It took me nearly ten years to attend a service there, as I had assumed that this was just a typical church. At some point, I observed such high attendance that the streets surrounding my condo overflowed with cars, creating a parking problem each Sunday. I also noticed music pouring out of the sanctuary each Sunday, and I was finally intrigued enough to go in and see what all the fuss was about. The music ministry at this church immediately took me by surprise. The energy that it produced was intoxicating, which actually brought me back quite often thereafter. That was the hook, but that was not everything. It was the congregants and their open-mindedness that also got my attention. The minsters and congregants were all quite loving and nonjudgmental. Hugs were standard protocol for saying Hello each Sunday, kisses if you knew them personally.

During this time, I found a spiritual awakening and a newfound interpretation of the Bible that I had been missing all my life. It was a metaphysical interpretation, something I had never been exposed to before. To me, a metaphysical look at God, instead of the literal look I had known previously, made perfect sense to me. It nearly erased all of the negative and confusing ideas conveyed to me by the original Bible that I had been exposed to. Unity generally teaches not to take everything so literally, and when you succeed at taking all judgments out of the Bible, the stories become more meaningful and glorious when learned through the actual ministry of Jesus Christ.

This new path finally strengthened my understanding and love of God. It broke my consternation for God, and I have since found peace. My newfound enlightenment empowers me with an understanding that we are the Creators of our own thinking and destinies and should stop using others as a crutch, including God. We can easily tap into the power of positive thinking and the power of intention. We are Creators, with equal powers as our own Creator. We are "chips off the ol' block," so to speak. Jesus attempted to convey that message to us, so very long ago.

I have come to realize that it is up to us to save ourselves, not God. My life until that point found it far too easy to place the blame on life's problems outside myself, and of course, God was always a perfect scapegoat. I began to learn that I could connect with God without praising Him for all the good and without condemning Him for all the bad. I was getting closer to Him by becoming nonjudgmental. What a concept! Loving what is, regardless of circumstance! Yet I would not be very authentic if I did not admit to finding fault or expressing criticism of what I find negative to our well-being, which you probably picked up on when I was relaying my issues with our political system. Yet we would be far better off if we did less complaining about what is not working and more campaigning for what is working. Okay, so that sounds a little "Mother Teresa–esque," I admit it, but it seems she was correct all those years ago.

Divine Intervention?

When I was a young man, I wanted to believe in God and the divine here on Earth. After all, I do believe in angels to a certain degree, and I could say a Holy Spirit makes perfect sense. However, do I believe that such spirits can impregnate a human being? I don't know, but I doubt it. It would seem that the spiritual world can only interact with the physical world on a spiritual level through our connected Source Energy, the one thing we share. Not everyone can connect to a Holy Spirit, because it is not physical. I surmise that it is equivalent to how radio waves work. While invisible, we still know they exist, but we can only receive them if we are in the right place and have the correct conduit (receiver). We must also know the correct frequency for it to reach us in the physical sense, and only then can they be translated by the receiver, in this case our eardrums. The alignment of the stars must be perfect. Every human has the capacity but not always the ability.

I think of the spiritual world as a realm where angels and master souls interact as a healing conduit for humans to stay in touch with God, again, through a Holy Spirit, one might say. However, staying in touch is on a level that is not physical. What if this is why prayer, for some of us, feels so powerful. Couldn't it be extraordinary contact with the divine on a spiritual level? What if, through prayer and meditation, we tap into another dimension of space-time where clarity and knowledge abounds? Through prayer, we can get a sense of some relief from life's physical troubles and miseries, because we can get an unadulterated understanding of that which we are praying, and thus, get some clarity. Through prayer and meditation, and while focusing on our breathing, we can quiet our minds from all the clutter of life's dramas. This brings us peace.

Understand that while angels and master souls may have contact with us, they may or may not have direct contact with God. And while they are transcended - or transitioned - beings, they are still stuck in our same illusionary world, albeit on a different level. The difference between the spiritual and physical realms is more than mortal contrast; most of the spiritual realm knows this world is an illusion, while most of us in the physical realm do not. The biggest difference is those in the spiritual realm understand the true nature of our separation from God and only wishes to ease our pain. Their reason for communicating with us, and perhaps influencing us, is a loving reminder that we are still children of the almighty and that He is just waiting for us to awaken from our dream, or nightmare. They perhaps feel that when contact is necessary, it is to calm our human anxiety and settle our fears. While we think we are in touch with God, it is only vicarious contact through a holy conduit or transcended master, and so we feel connected to Him. There is certainly nothing wrong with that, as long as we are truthful about our illusions.

But getting back to divine intervention. I continue to admit my sincere doubts about this account in the Holy Bible. Physically, to conceive a child, you need spermatozoa, and without that, there can be no "immaculation" (I made that word up, but you catch my drift). There is no such thing as magic, for there is always an underlying physical explanation. Even miracles are nothing more than the power of extreme focus and intention with very physical results. Therefore, there must be a human father of some kind.

What if Jesus's creation was the result of one of the first artificial insemination procedures? Perhaps. Is it possible that the virgin mother, Mary, was abducted by alien beings and impregnated artificially? Maybe. But for what purpose? There could be some kind of genetic explanation, but without Jesus's DNA, we will never know. Suffice it to say that Jesus was an amazing human being, but he was only more special than you or I because he was enlightened to our true nature by tapping into divine knowledge. Very few of us have mastered this, which makes humans like Jesus all the more special. There is no doubt that Jesus demonstrated extraordinary human powers through his powers of intention. What if the people of the time felt compelled to exemplify Jesus for his incredible capabilities by deeming him the Messiah? Remember: human beings like to have explanations for miraculous events, and making him our Savior was probably the most logical justification of the time. Besides, there was already a story written about a Messiah, and they needed to be saved. What was needed was the actor to play the part, and without realizing it, Jesus unwittingly stepped right into that role.

What makes Jesus stand out in my mind was his understanding and connection to God. He understood that we must resign from our adherence to this alternate reality in order to return to His kingdom in Heaven. He understood that we must forgive ourselves for straying and creating this physical world of contrast. After we forgive ourselves, we can more easily forgive the transgressions of our fellow human beings, and love will abound while we are here playing our human roles.

But I believe Jesus also knew that fellow humans need to be guided to this conclusion through teachings of parables and examples we can understand. Expecting anything else would be like having Einstein try and explain relativity and then expecting us to understand quantum mechanics. This kind of information is at a level that is outside most of our understandings, so it had to be dealt with carefully. Still, Jesus's words were considered blasphemy, because what did get around was somewhat incomprehensible to most and his ideas were so far astray from the mainstream he had to be labeled a heretic.

Does it really matter whether Jesus was born out of divine intervention? Would it make the man less holy if there was no immaculate conception? As I stated in my introduction, doesn't a rose by any other name smell as sweet? Wouldn't Jesus's example be just as honorable? Wouldn't his teachings be just as deep and memorable? Wouldn't his love shown for all things living be just as powerful? Regardless of how Jesus came into the world, my own Christ consciousness leads me to forgiveness which allows me to express more love for those I come into contact with. My Christ consciousness allows me to be a better man, a better *hu-man*, that is. But to be human is to also be fallible, and so was Jesus. He lost his temper on occasion when he saw injustices around him, just as we all do from time to time. It is easy to get caught up in the drama of life on Earth.

The ultimate question that most "spiritual" (non-atheist) human beings may ask before the end of their human existence is, how do I return to God?

The only reason the human spirit has such a difficult time getting back to Heaven is due to a strong attachment to the physical self. And I say *physical self* because most of us really believe that we are our human bodies. We have identified ourselves with our bodies, soon after birth, because we identify with the pain of existing in human form. That pain seems very real, and so begins the cementing of the illusion. So totally do we think we are our bodies that we can hardly let go of them when our times come to make a transition. Society has us programmed to believe that we are human. I mean, after all, what do we see when we look in the mirror? We think we see who we are, and yet it is nothing but a shell that we created.

I cannot stress enough that we only adopted the human being to carry out our will while in the physical realm. We came to play. We needed a physical form to play in, the human being turned out to be the best subject for this, end of story. It is hard to shed this attachment that we have with the body adoptive. Yet there are some that do understand the facade. Do you ever wonder why some people, whether in a traumatic accident or from natural causes, die so quickly, so easily, and so peacefully? It is because they have an epiphany, or understanding, that their true selves are not the bodies they have associated with for so many years. When they do realize the truth, it is easy to let go and transition. Perhaps they realize, "I'm through with that body. Next!"

But then there are some who hold on till the very tragic end. It should not be difficult to understand that they perhaps believe that this is all there is and their bodies are what keep them in the world of the living. Or there could be loved ones who are keeping them here, keeping them from their peaceful transitions because of both their own selfish attachment to the one they love and their simple inability to let go of them. They think the person they love is that body. If you truly love someone, you must let go of him or her when it is that person's time, not when it is your time to let go of them.

The truth of the matter is, until we can totally disassociate with the physical world (the human body included), we are destined to come back to that which we associate with, through various incarnations, until we understand that it is a choice that we can reject. Some believe that we come back (reincarnate) until we are "sin-free." The true sin we carry, if any, is the strong attachment we have to this world, which is a false world or false reality. Believing in this world is the sin. When we attach our mind to this world we connect with Ego which directs our actions in it. Such actions are usually contrary to the will of God. Once we understand that this is a false world, we will be able to escape from Ego and the bonds we created in it, and we will return to our true home in Heaven. Until then, we are destined to stay here, apart and seemingly separated from God. Coming back, over and over again, is like that *Twilight Zone* horror I described earlier, and at some point we will decide when we've had enough and get off the merry-go-round of life on planet Earth.

Our Father, who art in Heaven, is still in Heaven, awaiting our return. Understand that while you may see God in everything around us, He is not. He is not vested in our dream of this planet and would not subscribe to it. He would not and cannot participate in its illusionary existence and would rather we wake from this dream and reunite with Him. The sooner we stop believing in this fantasy world, the sooner we will be home with Him!

Oh, What Yin and Yang Have We?

Even Chinese philosophy holds that opposite forces may be, in fact, complementary. We normally think of opposites in terms of contradiction, but it seems this is a more natural state than one might imagine, one of equilibrium and balance. It is, afterall, our world of contrast. Time and space make this difficult to see at times, but this force of nature shows up in our behaviors and attitudes toward many things in life.

It's hard to see that all things balance out, eventually. The frustration that most people have is that the balancing doesn't seem to happen quick enough. One thing is for sure: there will always be good and evil, right and wrong, strong and weak; it always depends upon your perspective. To the thousands of souls who support the recent Islamic caliphate, they see their objective as a cleansing of their religion, while most all other religions look on with disgust and view Islam as being hijacked by a few radicals. Most see this "holy war" as something evil, destructive, and sinister. However, one could argue that the Western interventionist model is an unjust interference in many societies around the world, where many thousands of innocent lives have been wasted as a consequence of such influences or nation building. "Collateral damage," they are referred to, as if not human deaths but only the destruction of inanimate objects. Yet this is unfortunately not new in human history.

History is replete with cycles of violence, destruction, and of brutal dictators. Hitler, Hideki Tojo, Pol Pot, Genghis Khan, Mao Zedong, Vlad the Impaler, Vladimir Lenin, Joseph Stalin, Leonid Brezhnev, (Bloody) Nicholas II, Mao Tse-Tung, Idi Amin, Saddam Hussein, Kim il-Sung, Kim Jong-il, and now, Kim Jong-un, are a handful of history's most brutal and murderous leaders.

And more recently we have Vladimir Putin of Russia who was found to have ordered the poisoning of his opponents on multiple occasions, and Crown Prince Mohammed bin Salman of Saudi Arabia who was found to have ordered the dismemberment of an American Journalist in order to silence their criticisms. You would think that this would be unheard of in the 21st Century but think again. In reality, there are very few countries that are immune from the taint of such arrogance and evil intent. Who or what gives anyone the right to have dominion over another? Who or what gives any government or religion preference over another? The fact is, the human experiment is completely flawed due to such arrogant beliefs that any one person or any one religion or any one form of government is better than another. The arrogance is found everywhere, to the extent that many believe that "my way of life is the only way, sanctioned by the Almighty [whatever that might be], and if you do not adhere to my way of life, then I have the right to eliminate you!" Such beliefs have been the underlying source of all wars throughout our short history on this planet, and responsible for the taking of hundreds of millions of lives in the process.

Like every good fairytale, it seems that eventually, good triumphs over evil. But that is also just a false perception. In reality, it is all just part of a larger cycle that must coexist. In a world of contrast, you cannot have one without the other. Contrast mandates Yin and Yang and that both good and evil exist simultaneously, and the cycle we see is that one usually dominates over another for a period. In a shared balance of power, albeit shared at different times, these seemingly opposing forces swing like a pendulum. It is in this natural balance that gives rise to our humanity. We must believe that good will triumph over evil, but it is never easy because much energy exists on both ends of the scale, and the power of attraction will always prevail.

A world of contrast must have the Yin and Yang of good and bad, black and white, soft and hard, good and evil, life and death. Our perceptions of this balance is dependent upon our programming, perhaps beginning as early as birth. We can be taught that violence is a natural response to injustice or that peace and benevolence is mightier than the sword. The circumstances in which we find ourselves often depend upon where we are born and to whom. Our exposures in life at an early age usually dictates our attitudes later in life, dependent upon whether we are born into poverty or lives of luxury. Whether we are taught that only the strong survive, or the righteous will prevail, we get our programming from various sources. It can be taught to us by our parents, through religious beliefs, or by the government under which we find ourselves ruled by. We are programmed to take such beliefs seriously, and oftentimes threaten with deadly consequences should we prove adversarial. One only need look at dictatorships such as North Korea or Russia, or religious militant groups such as Al-Qaeda and Daesh (or ISIL), where you are likely to be killed or "disappeared" should you oppose their authority or rule of law. No trial, no sentencing, here one minute gone the next – poof, no more opposition. And many cultures and societies on this planet do not believe in freedom of the press or free speech. And many authors and journalists practicing free speech often pay a high price for voicing their opinions – retribution and even death. This makes it all the more difficult to understand, even hypocritical, for any society to do business with cultures or governments that may be considered barbaric in this modern global age. But we are often told there is a bigger picture to consider and to overlook the hypocrisy. When you are raised with such freedoms, it is difficult to imagine other cultures who forbid the same. Some forbid women to interact with men or do not allow women the right to vote, while some even prevent girls from attending school. The 15-year-old Pakistani girl, Malala Yousafzai, shot in the head by the Taliban for pursuing her right to learn, is only one of many examples in recent times. Thankfully, she survived to tell her story.

But sometimes the pendulum can swing too fast for society to accept. The seemingly archaic and puritanical attitudes still found in the United States today, for example, appear to have fought back against the liberal mind-set that the United States has enjoyed over the past decade or so. As evidenced in the recent election, it would appear that the pendulum has swung in favor of conservatives, to the degrees that many new freedoms we have witnessed are at risk of being reversed. One might say its Yin and Yang at its best. So if you get enough people riled up about the status quo, you might find a revolt, even in the tamest and democratic of societies. And the balance of power may be seen to shift once again.

Loving what is oftentimes proves challenging when something goes against your core beliefs. But love it we must, for the endurance of Yin and Yang cannot be stopped. It is a force of nature. It is an integral part of our world of contrast. And when we push too hard against that which we are opposed, we oftentimes give that which we are opposed more energy. Remember, the power of attraction does not understand you are opposed to a thing, it only understands that you are calling upon more energy with that vibration. It is therefore better to call upon more energy in the wake of what you wish to achieve, not against that which you do not, for energy is energy, regardless of its intended purpose. This is the universal law of attraction.

CHAPTER 9

What if all living creatures in our world have souls?

Do Animals Have Souls?

As the Universe expands and things multiply, so do we. This is at the heart of our creation story. We create through our power of intention, and we multiply. We souls take on those things as we see fit to experience through. Our most popular host is, of course, the human being, but we can choose to take on the form of almost anything we like.

The point is, and to make it perfectly clear, I am of the strong belief that all animals on our planet have souls, because we can and do experience contrast through them as well. So don't let anyone or anything, including any written sacred texts, imply that animals do not have souls, for that would contradict our purpose here.

The problem we may have with admitting that all things worldly can carry souls may be in our thinking that we have dominion over them. If you agree that killing another human being is murder, it is precisely because that human has a soul. Isn't your pet a being also? Just because you are attached to your pet, as opposed to it living in the wild, does not negate the fact that they each have a soul. Therefore, once you agree that animals have a soul, you might admit that killing them is also murder. This is a complex proposition, because you might question if one soul should then have dominion over another? The reason this question is tough to reconcile is when thinking of carnivores.

If an animal has a soul and it is killed for food, whether naturally in the animal kingdom or by humans, you still need to consider that act to be murder if you believe that human killings are murder. Think about that for a minute. You cannot cherry-pick this act. If you tend to agree, then you may also wish to admit that you are completely hooked in this physical world of existence, and you most probably identify with this life of contrast far too much to be able to separate from it. This idea is very important when considering how to return home to God. You will not be able to return home to God if you are stuck in this false reality and completely identify in it. The journey home depends upon giving this false life up. I will speak more on this in the final chapter, but it is fundamental to your understanding of the truth of who you are.

In order for you to reconcile this premise, you must agree that these lives are not who we are, and we souls are merely hitchhikers. Consider our bodies like the vehicles we drive. They are only intended to get us around this life of contrast. Killing a living thing is not murder because we hitchhikers can simply move on to a new one. Remember: the physical body that is killed, whether human or animal is just a temporary vehicle for the soul that occupies it. But make no mistake about it: if you kill my body, I think I would be unhappy because my soul may not have been done with it yet. I may be enjoying this life of contrast and feel I have more to experience and learn from. If you kill me, you won't harm the real me, but you will disrupt my involvement that I came here to experience. So please don't kill me. I have more to experience here and the termination of my physical body is not one of them. I do not wish to start over.

And so, we may think of all life in this world the same way. Their souls may not wish to terminate their experience yet. So killing a living thing, while it may not be murder, it may be completely inconvenient to terminate the host it's being used for. I know this sounds extreme, but as long as you continue to identify with your host body, you will not be able to let go when your host ends its useful life. As long as you cannot let go, you will be stuck to come back to this world of contrast and go through another iteration, albeit in a different life form. It's completely up to you.

Suffice to say that humans, and all animal life forms in this world, and actually in the entire universe, have a purpose to host our souls in order for us to experience a life of contrast, nothing more.

The Power of What If?

The bottom line is that anything in this Universe is possible. We could ask what if, followed by any question about any topic, and the answer can always be aligned with "yes, that is quite possible." If enough energy is put towards an intention, it can be accomplished.

If the proposition to the answer is compelling enough, we humans will go to extraordinary lengths to explore and prove it, even if only a theory. The tools created to prove a theory have oftentimes ended up to be marvelous achievements in and of themselves.

Innovation, through our energy and willingness to create or invent, is always spawned by our what-if questions. If we did not ask, "What if such and such were possible?" technologies would never result. The moment human beings began to imagine what it would be like to have or do something was the dawn of technology and advancement. At that moment, our intelligence grew as we gained more knowledge about life and the world around us. Our health improved because we began experimenting from the what-if ideas of helping fix injuries and other health-related problems. Cultures were created by recording and handing down what we learned, and societies grew from the cultures established where tribes and communities could live more harmoniously. We realized early on in our evolution that sharing and helping one another had an exponential effect to our own benefit. We soon realized the enormous power of our what-if questions. As such, our souls thrive in our experiences here. Humans thrive, our pets thrive, all creatures seen and unseen thrive because this is our purpose.

CHAPTER 10

What if our dream of contrast is actually a nightmare?

Dream or Nightmare

Many people might go so far as to say this life is a nightmare. If you are one of the 783 million people in the world who do not have access to clean water and among the 2.5 billion who do not have access to adequate sanitation[45], you might be one who believes we are living in a nightmare. If you are one in nine people on Earth, you would be one of 795 million people in the world who do not have enough food to lead a healthy active life[46], and you might think you are living in a nightmare. If you are one of the 1,685,000 new cases of cancer diagnosed in the United States last year, or one of 14 million people worldwide with the same diagnosis, you might think you are living in a nightmare. If you were a family, friend, or loved one of the nearly 13,000 gun murders in the United States last year, you might think you are living in a nightmare. I could go on and on, but you get the notion.

The truth of the matter is the world that we created is not a perfect place. It is not as pretty as we would like, and it never will be. No matter how close we get to create a utopia here on Earth, there never will be one. Perfection is a moving target, and contrast dictates extremes to keep this constantly in motion. We will always have wars and terrorists and people who are unhappy with their circumstances. History is replete with those who want to blame someone else for their unhappiness and misery, and they will inflict pain and suffering outward as a response. These are the many prices we must pay for contrast. Utopia and perfection can only exist in a place of no place, without boundaries and without conditions, and absolutely cannot have contrast. Many people call this place of no place *Heaven.*

It is a fact that there is quite a bit of suffering all around us here in America but even more so in most of the underdeveloped parts of the world. Add to that how bleak our way of life may become, should global warming and the affects from climate change continue to threaten us, and they will.

Crops are failing and droughts are creating another dust bowl in the Midwest. Each year, wildfires outnumber the year before. In 2015 over 10 million acres burned in the United States alone. An extra foot of sea level has been added in this past century, and this may not yet account for the effects from all the additional greenhouse gases that has been added in recent years. The increasing routine of tidal flooding is already making life miserable in places like Miami Beach Florida, Charleston South Carolina, and Norfolk Virginia, even on sunny days[47]. Though these types of floods from rising tides often produce only a foot or two of standing seawater, they are straining life in many towns by killing lawns and trees, blocking neighborhood streets and clogging storm drains, polluting supplies of freshwater, and sometimes stranding entire island communities for hours by overtopping the roads that tie them to the mainland. Such events are just an early harbinger of the coming damage the newest research suggests.

One quote that hits home from Washington state governor Jay Inslee, *"We are the first generation to experience climate change and the last generation that can do something about it!"*[48] Even Pope Francis is quoted as saying, *"If I may use a strong word, I would say we are at the limits of suicide!"*[49] I guess you could say we are to blame. And you could say, we have to take the good with the bad. The bottom line is we need to be prepared for anything, especially if it is already too late. Rising sea levels will leave up to 760 million people homeless, according to estimates from scientific research organization Climate Central. And article found at Discovery. com, entitled, 760 Million Displaced by Rising Sea Levels, goes on to say, *"Should global temperature rise by 4 degrees Celsius, global sea levels will accordingly rise up to 35 feet, submerging the homes of 10% of the world's population."*[50]

There are many reasons why so many Americans believe that climate change is a hoax. While a few just do not believe in the science being shown, the simple truth is that fear keeps the hoax alive. Deep down the deniers know it is really happening, but there are many credible scientists also reporting that it is already too late; it is too late to reverse what is happening, so why cause a panic? Their answer is of course then to deny, deny, deny! It will be denied as long as possible in order postpone change and perhaps to save money and/or widespread panic.

But nightmares are only as real as we give them energy and attention. Dwelling on our Earthly problems will not change them. But focusing on solutions can. At least, stopping our assault on the planet's ecosystem can help and, if done in a unified way, may reverse the negative effects we've had on it as a species. We do impact our physical experiences, but we also have the power to choose their relevance to our true nature. We can choose how much drama they will cause in our lives as humans. While we are here having fun in our experiences, it is only natural for us to try and make it as pleasing as possible. We are here to have fun and experience as much joy as possible. Even if it's only a false reality, we are here to purposely take part in its falsehood, because this is what we intended. We are not here by accident!

Our Final Judgment

When we look back at this crazy and at times exciting life that we created in this alternate reality, we will finally remember that all we wanted to do was to create contrast, to better understand our place in Heaven. That desire or wanting is why we created our world and our subsequent ride in it. But as every runaway child will do, we will finally grow tired of discomfort and desire to go home, and we will realize that this dream came from our potential to wonder (and wander). We will remember our place in Heaven and that our potential for pure bliss can never be achieved here during this dream on this planet where only suffering may prevail.

Nevertheless, many people have a problem with the idea of no judgment day. They feel that those who have wronged another human being should be punished. They are caught up in the age-old cycle of right and wrong, of judgment and punishment. If they could only understand that God has no desire and no need for judgment and punishment, they might adopt the same Godlike quality themselves.

Rather than accepting the idea for a judgment day to be the wrath of God, as the Bible suggests, we should instead bask in the peaceful understanding that the undeniable love of God will be our homecoming. We have nothing to fear. We really have done nothing wrong. We were innocent children, playing, and then wandered into this dream. Okay, so we lost our way, oops! God is just waiting for us to awaken from this dream that we find ourselves in, and like the biblical story of the Prodigal Son, our Father will rejoice in our return home, for it will be a reunion like no other!

Of all the parables found in the Holy Bible, the Prodigal Son is my all-time favorite. It is probably the nearest and dearest to me, because it was told by Jesus Christ himself. It recognizes human frailty and mortal bad judgment. It is truly a story of love and redemption and, most of all, forgiveness without judgment or condemnation. The older brother in the story is as perplexed by the father's reaction of love and good will, just as the people are that I mentioned in the previous illustration. But the brother cannot be criticized for his disdain for he was obviously programmed by society to feel the need to judge and punish, just as we have been programmed. Understand that it is society's need to judge and punish, not the father. Likewise, God, cannot and would not scold us or judge us. We are His beloved, and we have done nothing wrong. We most certainly will be reunited in love, peace, comfort, and joy!

Shaking the bonds of this physical dream world that we created will not be easy. We have completely identified with it. When we look in the mirror, we think we see who we truly are, but what we see staring back at us is only a reflection of physical beings that we conjured up (adopted) to get us through this lifetime of smoke and mirrors. The cycle is repeated through consecutive lifetimes in what many call *reincarnation*. Our mind (or spirit body) simply reanimates in a new corporeal body. We recognize our inner spirits but have difficulty identifying with them, because they lack contrast.

Remember: our entire purpose in this dream was a desire for contrast, and as long as we remain focused on that and everything physical, we cannot fully connect with our true selves and leave this phony existence behind. As long as we identify with the physical instead of the spiritual, we are bound here with the chains of servitude.

The good news is that we will not be bound for an eternity. At some point, we will have had enough, and we will break the chains that bind us here. ACIM can provide an avenue out, but it will take determination and a willingness to abandon holding on to the values placed on everything physical in this world.

Our Return to God

What if getting back to Heaven simply means denying all relevance on Earth?

It is clear that a vast majority of the world's population believes in a God of some sort or another. Certainly, God plays heavily in the psyche of American culture. After all, the national Pledge of Allegiance to our country states that we are "One nation under God" and our federal currency imprints "In God We Trust" on every note and every coin. Yet the percentage of people who believe in God has been in decline here in the U.S. and across the globe. Why is this occurring? Contrary to popular belief, it may not be because we feel more "spiritual" than "religious." It could be because technology has moved us away from His relevance, or maybe more and more people believe that God cannot be part of this madness, and they are looking for another answer.

It is thought by many that we have entered into an enlightened age. As human intelligence increases with technology, global awareness, and with more connectivity and collaboration, we tend to rely less on the intangible and more on the tangible – logical - experience for knowledge. This may be why the masses are having less religious faith than just a century ago. Fewer and fewer people participate in organized religion, which relies on having faith in something that is commonly believed to be true or real. They may expect actual evidence instead of having faith in what is being preached. It is this shift where you see more people saying, "Prove it!"

Fewer people are likely to believe something as gospel just because an ancient book says it to be so. They want hard evidence in this techno-world. Personally, I would sooner believe that an alien from some far-off physical world abducted and then impregnated the mother of Jesus Christ than would I believe that a divine spirit or God intervened. Why? Because at least an alien being is something tangible to consider that might have the physical technology to fertilize a human embryo. And, if such an "extraterrestrial visit" did take place, wouldn't it be more likely that any witnesses would have assumed it was a divine visitation? Wouldn't the interpretation have been of a Heavenly Godlike nature? I'm not saying the authors of the New Testament were fooled by something that seemed miraculous, for such a visitation would have been miraculous even in today's world. I'm saying it is more likely that it was an extraordinary visit by a superior being – or beings - with an agenda. The intelligence of the people at the time simply assumed it was God's intervention. It was the only interpretation they could come up with. And once again, they had a prophecy they could "fulfill" to fit what occurred. And maybe, just maybe, Jesus enlightenment was also knowledge brought to him with an extraterrestrial origin. It makes sense if you believe we humans have had help surviving in this world. By giving us more knowledge and technology, possibly through an "enlightenment gene," extraterrestrial beings could be simply trying to help us. Of course the question would be, what's the motive?

Perhaps, by selecting good candidates for enlightenment, the masses can be better educated. These so-called extraterrestrials could very well be our own species from the future, circling back to give mankind a boost. I'm just sayin, anything is possible!

Understandably, most organized religious institutions of the Christian faith would proclaim such line of thinking to be sacrilegious or heretical. But there are many who have trouble with the so-called divine intervention story. And now that I believe we exist in an illusionary realm, created by 'us' for our own purpose, it does not seem sacrilegious for me to make this claim.

Forgiveness

What keeps us stuck in this Universe (this physical world), preventing our return to God, is this notion that God created this world we live in. If you worship God and believe He lives among us here on Earth, then it follows that you would be married to this physical existence in order to stay connected to Him. It is worth repeating that as long as we continue a notion that Heaven and God are of this world, we will remain stuck here, because we will not want to leave it. In order to escape the trap that we have created, a person must completely dismiss (by true forgiveness) the notion that we separated from God in the first place. When we practice our true natures as love in expression, when we accept that this world is but a dream that we fell into, and when we forgive ourselves for creating this alternate reality, we will then shed the bonds that bind us to this physical world. Dismissing this alternate reality will allow us to reunite with our loving God and awaken from the dream of the planet. This was the true nature of forgiveness that Jesus attempted to share with us long ago, it was the cornerstone of his ministry on Earth.

The Foundation for a Course in Miracles goes further by saying,

> *Forgiveness is unknown in* Heaven, *where the need for it would be inconceivable. However, in this world, forgiveness is a necessary correction for all the mistakes that we have made. To offer forgiveness is the only way for us to have it, for it reflects the law of* Heaven *that giving and receiving are the same. Heaven is the natural state of all the Sons of God as He created them. Such is their reality forever. It has not changed because it has been forgotten*[51].

It goes on to say,

> *Forgiveness is the means by which we will remember. Through forgiveness the thinking of the world is reversed. The forgiven world becomes the gate of Heaven, because by its mercy we can at last forgive ourselves. Holding no one prisoner to guilt, we become free. Acknowledging Christ in all our brothers, we recognize His Presence in ourselves. Forgetting all our misperceptions, and with nothing from the past to hold us back, we can remember God. Beyond this, learning cannot go. When we are ready, God Himself will take the final step in our return to Him.*

Judgment Day

I hate to burst the bubble of certain religious zealots and many of my Christian brothers and sisters, but **there will be no judgment day**, if you will forgive yourself for taking part in this world. I know that will come as a great shock to many, but all tales of judgment day (to me) are false where they hold that God will be judging us. That "day" is not going to happen. The only judgment that may transpire when you transition your life on this planet will be your own self-judgment. If you have not forgiven yourself for everything you have done or not done, then you will stand in judgment of yourself—that is it. It will be a false judgment to say the least, but it will not be a judgment from God, period!

I understand why this lie has been proliferated throughout history, starting with the Holy Bible, and to a certain degree, there is a valid argument that can be made. When you understand that there will be no judgment day, you might think this would lead to complete lawlessness. Why? Because if God is not going to be there waiting for us at the holy gate in judgment of our lives, allowing us into Heaven (or not), then why would we need to worry about our behavior while we are alive on Earth? It is kind of like the theory that if we don't have police in our community, then there will be crime of all kinds, from theft to rape to murder. Gee, we have that with police in our communities now. Can you imagine if those deeds were not considered sins, and we did not have to worry about meeting our maker?

Herein lies the scare tactic of a "judgment day" that has been used for thousands of years. Religions in society must convince you that God is a vengeful God in order to keep your behavior in line. If you believe in God and have a conscience, you probably believe you will be judged by God when your time comes to pass. And you would not be alone; we have all been programmed to believe this.

Understandably, it is quite difficult for some people to reconcile this concept of no judgment day in their minds. They ask, "So when a murderer gets to Heaven, would they be treated with the same love and open arms as someone who has never wronged another soul in his or her life?" And the answer is *yes*, because the wrongs we have decided to label and harbor here in this physical, illusory world have no consequence in Heaven, just like what happens in your dreams at night have no consequence on what happens after you awaken from that dream. When we finally awaken from this physical hallucination, all misgivings in this dream disappear just as they do each night when you awaken to start each new day on Earth, which is only a continuation of this larger dream that we had the power to manifest so long ago.

So the seemingly hideous ideas that we can physically do or perceive to do to one another, like murder, rape, incest, and so on, need to be forgiven, just like all other worldly tragedies and natural disasters. Just the same as understanding the acts in our nightly dreams are not real. We do not need to forgive the act; we only need to forgive the dream of them. The only difference between what we do in this physical dream and what we do in the ethereal dreams (those we have when we sleep) is that we are convinced the physical dream is real. It is the reason we keep coming back to it. The process of getting back to Heaven is undoing this belief, because this is not the truth of who we are. We must forgive ourselves for not thinking outside the box of this physical world.

Again, please understand, there will be no judgment day, at least not by God, because God is not part of our dream here and has no interest in intervening or interjecting in it. Besides, I have already established that it is not in God's nature to judge. Even if He were of this world, God has no need to judge. God is always loving what is, but this life and this reality is not of God, it is our story, it is our dream, and God has no part in it. A good question might be; what if God felt the same need that we did to create contrast? And a good answer might be then that He is part of this story, this illusion. Since I believe God has no interest or need for contrast, I conclude He also does not take part of it.

I would imagine that at his level of existence God might see this as a silly whimsical need of ours and perhaps sees his children as simply out playing. We, not God, are the authors, the producers, the directors, and, of course, the star actors in this unfolding drama we call "a life of contrast." This movie, this dream, this perceived reality is ours alone. If we wish to return home to God, we must take ownership and accept that this world is not the truth of who we are as God's children, and this world has no integrity with God. When we are tired of the struggle and the conflicts created out of this dream and we can forgive ourselves for dreaming it in the first place, then and only then will we have no need to justify it and give evidence to it and we will have no need to continue with it. In that instant, we will finally be home together with our Father, and we will carry on in true bliss.

One of the most heralded and famous film critics, Roger Ebert, is quoted as saying, "And so on this (final) day of reflection, I say thank you for going on this journey with me; I'll see you at the movies!" I think his words are very poignant, because that is truly what this reality is—just a movie that we created for ourselves. And we have bought into this "movie of life" as reality, right from the start, from the moment of our conception of this idea.

Think about that for a moment: conception. We are merely a concept, a construct of an idea to gain perspective through contrast, as I have said in the beginning of this writing. We believe everything that plays out before us is real when, in fact, we are just confused actors in the movie. It is difficult to conceive that we are both the actor and director, not to mention the producer and editor and so on. We are so caught up in this drama of life on Earth that we have lost all sense to what is real. The only things that may be considered real are our souls or spirits, which only exists to experience - to perceive - the intention behind everything we have created. Without our souls, we would have no intent, and the Universe would not exist. This may seem confusing but it is analogous to the philosophical question "If a tree falls in a forest and no one is around to hear it, does it make a sound?" The tree falling does not make a sound because sound is a byproduct of our perception validating it, for hearing it, therefore, if there is no one there to perceive the compression of air created by the tree hitting the ground, to actually "hear it", then it is only a vibration of an air wave that also cannot be evidenced. The same can be said for our souls, which only exist for the purpose of experiencing all of the contrast that we had created. This world of matter is our intention and without the intent, there would be no purpose for our souls to exist to perceive this world of contrast in the first place. Our souls are perceivers and are required to carry on the dream of the planet. Our souls are also needed for reincarnation because one human lifetime is not equivalent to the life span for this seemingly never ending story.

We Never Really Die!

In closing, I have tried to illustrate that, we are more than our physical bodies, and, while we do have a Creator, that Heavenly Father or God is not of this world. We are here to play and to experiment and to experience all the contrast that we had imagined. Again, our Heavenly Father knows we are off playing in a dream and is simply waiting for us to wake up and be present in His love and bliss. I say God is waiting, but I am not sure if waiting is applicable in a place of no time or space. It could very well be that our lifetimes here make up a mere fraction of existence in Heaven and so it is likely, then, that God is hardly missing us at all.

Because God is not of this world, we physical beings are on our own here. We cannot blame God or anyone else for the horrors we may witness through our countless lifetimes on this planet, nor should we give thanks and praise to God for all the beauty and wondrous matter that we created, unless you wish to thank Him for creating us with that ability. When I pray, I do give thanks and praise to God for *me* and my abilities to create in this world. And when I see things not so wonderful, I look around at how I might have attracted that into my life, not looking to blame anything for it. I strive to take responsibility for what we have and what we give, and trust that God had nothing to do with it. You must see that God is innocent of this false reality.

If only more of us could understand this concept, then perhaps we would live more joyous lives while we are here. Just because we grow up and become adults does not mean we should lose our innocence and stop playing, but in playing we must do so responsibly and conscientiously, treating all fellow human beings with the respect and dignity that we expect for ourselves. High-profile avatars, especially Jesus the Christ, the prophet Moses, Gautama the Buddha, the prophet Muhammad, and so on, have shared this ideal very succinctly through our world's recorded history. I believe we should follow their example. I also believe that most of these avatars understood that we (our souls) live on forever, so we must cherish and protect that sacredness by acting in good faith, always.

Therefore, since this world, or alternate reality, was conjured up in the first place, we cannot actually die. Just as in our dreams, it is not possible for us to actually die. Instead, we will eventually wake up. The only real difference is, in this dream world in which we find ourselves, we are on a different, more intricate, matrix than our dream-state during slumber, which are completely divorced from the reality we know in our waking states. Our association with our physical bodies and physical world is so complex that most of us find it difficult, if not impossible, to awaken from it. It's kind of like a merry-go-round that we can't seem to get off. Again, the reason is because we are so invested in this false reality that we are 100 percent convinced it is real. We will only awaken from it when we understand, just as we do in our nightly dreams during slumber, that it is not real.

I am sure that you have been in the midst of a bad dream at night and immediately snapped out of it because you subconsciously knew at some point that it was not real. The moment that we decide that this life is not the truth of who we are, we will snap out of it and wake up. As you might expect, that will simply take the form of not reincarnating and coming back here. This is precisely what must take place in the current reality we find ourselves in.

Sure, it is true that we hijacked Homo sapiens so that we could live in this physical realm and so that we could function at a higher level. And it is true that these corporeal bodies do have limited shelf lives. In this physical realm, our Earthly bodies eventually give out as they age and decay. It often appears, if left to live a ripe old age, that we eventually go back to whence we came immediately after birth—pretty much defenseless and dependent upon another adult to take care of us, that is, until we expire. But it is only an end to the physical vehicle we have been using here, not our true selves. All living things in this alternate reality eventually expire, as this outcome is the cost of having contrast. In fact, it is assumed the Universe itself has a shelf life. And while most of us cannot fathom that the Universe will ever end, it will eventually run out of energy, just as a star runs out of energy when it turns into a supernova or white dwarf. This is the price that has to be paid for a life of contrast. But our true selves, our spiritual energy, that part of us that still has its hooks in the nonphysical realm and resides with God right now, can never die. We are eternal, perpetual souls, in actuality. In that true reality, we have no corporal bodies and so there is nothing that can expire.

The less we identify with our corporal being here, the more we come in touch with our spiritual being. I call this, releasing and letting go. You will see this in many cultures, especially in Buddhism, Sikhism and Taoism. The trick to returning home to Heaven is completely divesting our thoughts from the untrue self of our physical bodies and of this physical world. This will be a monumental challenge for many of us. However, once we do, we can awaken from this dream. Until then, we are forced to relive in this life of contrast, over and over and over until we finally realize we've had enough. When we no longer associate with this world, with this dream, and no longer have use for all the goodies of its content and contrast in it, we will be home in an instant with God. And our Father will rejoice and throw a spiritual feast to celebrate our return, as the Prodigal Sons (and daughters) that we are, little lambs who truly did not know any better and only left His kingdom to go play. There will be no need for forgiveness as there is no right and wrong in Heaven, only pure love and joy, existing in true bliss. You see, we never really die. And as Abraham-Hicks so eloquently puts it:

> *We're not wanting to be insensitive to what so many of you are feeling, but we are very much wanting you to put this death thing in the proper perspective: You are all going to die! Except there is no death. You're all going to make your transition into Non-Physical. It is time to stop making your transition into Non-Physical sound like a subject that is uncomfortable and begin acknowledging that it is something that happens to everyone. This death thing is so misunderstood that you use it to torture yourself never-endingly and just absolutely unnecessarily. There are those who feel such fulfillment of life and such Connection to Source Energy, who understand that there is no separation between what is physical and Non-Physical; who understand that there is not even a lapse in consciousness, that "death" is a matter of closing one's eyes in this dimension and literally opening one's eyes in the other dimension. And that, truly, is how all death is, no matter how it looks, up to that point. The re-emergence into Source Energy is always a delightful thing.[52]*

So in this case, there are no "what if's", and's, or but's! We never really die. Our energy, spirit, or soul, simply changes focus back to our non-physical origins. And so it is, and so it shall be.

This book was written with much love. May you always be blessed with love peace and happiness!

Charlee

FEEDBACK

The author would love to hear your thoughts on this work. So, please feel free to email at: Charlee.Stardust@gmail.com. Thank you!

ACKNOWLEDGMENTS

First, to my personal friend Ioda who was a constant source of encouragement throughout this writing, for proofing the first drafts, and for finding grammatical errors for me to correct prior to the final editing. *Thank you!*

Second, to my beloved son Matt, who has been a great sounding board for me to bounce ideas off of. He is my closest friend and confidant and has a wisdom beyond his years. I always admire and respect and what he has to offer and include him in all my projects, big and small.

Third, there is a metaphorical expression that says, "You are what you eat." I interpret this to also mean, "You are what you read." Therefore, I would be remiss if I did not acknowledge the many influential authors of some very profound mind-altering books and essays that have opened my mind and touched my soul throughout my life. They have been my masters in many regards, and they are my other notable mentions.

Finally, there is our connection to our Source Creator; a God that does not exist in the physical realm but can surely exist in our spiritual domain. Our connections to our Creator can give us inspiration as well as bring us peace to an oftentimes chaotic physical world. And while the religions of the world attempt to bridge the gap we find that separates us from our Creator, they can also be seen to divide us more than they connect us. I owe many thanks to God as my underlying source of inspiration.

NOTABLE MENTIONS

Esther (and Jerry) Hicks who for decades have shared the universal wisdom of Abraham and for such insightful books as *The Law of Attraction, Ask and It Is Given,* and *The Vortex.*

Don Miguel Ruiz for his beautiful writings of *The Four Agreements, The Gift of Forgiveness,* and *The Mastery of Love.*

Byron Katie for The Work and her healing book *Loving What Is.*

Dr. Wayne Dyer for such inspirational books as *The Power of Intention, Change Your Thoughts - Change Your Life* and *Getting in the Gap.*

Eckhart Tolle for his profound works as *The Power of Now* and *A New Earth.*

Helen Schucman and William Thetford for *A Course in Miracles.*

Michael A. Singer for first enlightening me as a teenager with *The Search for Truth, Three Essays On Universal Law,* and later, *The Untethered Soul.*

Erich von Däniken, for opening my mind with the many "what if "questions presented in his work, Chariots of the Gods.

And last but certainly not least, my hero, Carl Sagan, for enlightening me as young adult with *Dragons of Eden: Speculations on the Evolution of Human Intelligence,* and later such works as *Broca's Brain: Reflections on the Romance of Science* and *The Varieties of Scientific Experience: A Personal View of the Search for God.*

I thank you all for adding a source of mystery and wonderment in my path of life!

What If explores and attempts to answer many of the questions each of us have thought of throughout our lives but may have been afraid to ask. Why am I here? Where did I come from? What created the universe? Which came first, the chicken or the egg?

Through many years of analysis and reflection, the author attempts the most logical conclusion of who we are, where we came from, our purpose for being, and more importantly, our relationship with our Creator. What If explores how our ego is primarily responsible for much of the negative dramas that play out in our lives; how the moment our egos began labeling things, we got into trouble; and how labeling turned into judgments and opinions. What If points to the fact that our purpose here on Earth is actually to enjoy the journey our life takes us on, and suggests ways to avoid the struggles and unhappiness that can easily interrupt us.

What If explores our world of form through our physical existence, and it helps us understand our more important beginnings in a place we might call heaven, in a nonphysical plane of existence. So get ready for a journey of discussions about subject matter that may be a little complex to entertain in our minds. What If helps smooth out kinks in those questions and hopes to give valid arguments for other more logical explanations.

"We are not meant to suffer, ever! We are meant to find joy in everything we experience. We were created from love and are meant to experience only love until we get back home!" The author.

With peace and love!

CREDITS, REFERENCES, AND FOOTNOTES

1 A multiverse, as defined by Wikipedia, is a hypothetical set of infinite possible Universes including the Universe which we live in. Source, /wiki/ Multiverse, Wikipedia.org.

2 This seemingly famous quote from Albert Einstein as referenced inquotes.net/quote/52742 article.

3 As quoted in a September 24, 2013 livescience.com article, "Why Catholic Priests Can't Marry."

4 *A Course in Miracles*, scribed by Helen Schucman and edited by William Thetford. Written from 1965 to 1972 and finally published in 1976.

5 According to biblehub.com, John 14:12.

6 Source, /wiki/Holy_Spirit, Wikipedia.org.

7 Carl Sagan, American astronomer, cosmologist, astrophysicist, astrobiologist, and best-selling author.

8 For the purposes of simplification, I do not make any distinction between the Ego and the Superego. F or our purpose here, they can be treated as one and the same.

9 According to biblehub.com, Matthew 7:1.

10 According to biblehub.com, John 8:7.

11 Reference Archery Terms at tumblr.com/search/archery%20terms.

12 Source: What It Says about A Course in Miracles, acim.org.

13 Quotation by W.C. Fields according to goodreads.com.

14 Quotation by Giorgio A. Tsoukalos, co-founder of *Legendary Times Magazine*.

15 Pulitzer Prize-winning book by Carl Sagan first published in 1977.

16 Source, /wiki/ Moore's_law, Wikipedia.org.

17 Charles Darwin's theory of evolution in the *On the Origin of Species*.

18 www.hhmi.org/news/human-brain-evolution-was-special-event.

19 Zecharia Sitchin was a Russian-born American author of books proposing an explanation for human origins involving ancient astronauts.

20 Source /wiki/Zecharia_Sitchin, Wikipedia.org.

21 Source, /wiki/Ur, Wikipedia.org.

22 *Law of Attraction* from best-selling authors Esther and Jerry Hicks (with Abraham), 2006.

23 *The Secret*, published in 2006 by Rhonda Byrne.

24 Source, /wiki/Esther_Hicks, Wikipedia.org.

25 *The Power of Intention*, published in 2005 by Dr. Wayne Dyer.

26 www.quoteinvestigator.com/category/thomas-edison/, from biography written in 1910.

27 Source, www.facebook.com/Abraham.Hicks/posts/572496479543678

28 Daily Quote September 27, 2015, excerpted from: Silver Spring, Maryland, on April 19, 1997.

29 As shared at www.azquotes.com.

30 The-science-behind-gratitude at hippy.com.

31 Excerpt from chapter 16 of *Ask and It Is Given*, the book by Esther and Jerry Hicks, as shared at abraham-hicks.com.

32 Taken from Wikipedia on Suffering.

33 Reference /wiki/Rainbow_Bridge_(pets) Wikipedia.org.

34 Thomas Carl "Thom" Hartmann is an American radio host, author, former psychotherapist, entrepreneur, and progressive political commentator. Source – Wikipedia.org.

35 Reference Wikipedia.org /wiki/History_of_slavery.

36 www.huffingtonpost.com/neha-misra/human-trafficking-a-big-b_b_2602398.html

37 www.globalslaveryindex.org/findings/

38 According to Snopes.com, "Happiness Is Only Grin Deep."

39 Reference - YouTube video promoting his book, *Jesus: Story of Enlightenment*.

40 Reference /wiki/Selfishness, Wikipedia.org.

41 From the book, *The Four Agreements*, Don Miguel Ruiz.

42 References to the Bible or the Holy Bible includes both Old and New Testaments unless otherwise specified.

43 The Lost Books of the Bible and the Forgotten Books of Eden and the Gospel of Mary Magdalene.

44 Quote from Rodney King after the LA Riots of 1992.

45 According to http://www.unwater.org.

46 According to www.wfp.org.

47 According to http://www.nytimes.com.

48 Source, www.newyorker.com/news/news-desk/last-chance-climate-change

49 Source, http://transcripts.cnn.com/TRANSCRIPTS/1607/27/ebo.01.html

50 Source,www.discovery.com/dscovrd/nature/climate-change-by-the-numbers-760-million-displaced-by-rising-sea-levels/

51 Source: What It Says about A Course in Miracles, acim.org.

52 Daily Quote - March 04, 2014, excerpted from: Buffalo, New York, on September 25, 2001.

Printed in the United States
By Bookmasters